101 best campsites
by the beach

alan rogers

Compiled by: Alan Rogers Guides Ltd

Designed by: Vine Design Ltd

© Alan Rogers Guides Ltd 2010

Published by: Alan Rogers Guides Ltd,
Spelmonden Old Oast, Goudhurst, Kent TN17 1HE

www.alanrogers.com
Tel: 01580 214000

British Library Cataloguing-in-Publication Data:
A catalogue record for this book is available from
the British Library.

ISBN 978-1-906215-34-7

Printed in Great Britain by
Stephens & George Print Group

contents

alanrogers.com/beach

Welcome to the Alan Rogers
'101' **guides**

The Alan Rogers guides have been helping campers and caravanners make informed decisions about their holiday destinations since 1968. Today, whether online or in print, Alan Rogers still provides an independent, impartial view, with detailed reports, on each campsite.

With so much unfiltered, unqualified information freely available, the Alan Rogers perspective is invaluable to make sure you make the right choice for your holiday.

What is the '101' **series**?

At Alan Rogers, we know that readers have many and diverse interests, hobbies and particular requirements. And we know that our guides, featuring a total of some 3,000 campsites, can provide a bewildering choice from which it can be difficult to produce a shortlist of possible holiday destinations.

The Alan Rogers 101 guides are devised as a means of presenting a realistic, digestible number of great campsites, featured because of their suitability to a given theme.

This book remains first and foremost an authoritative guide to excellent campsites which offer great seaside holidays.

101 **Best campsites by the beach**

For many, a holiday is not a holiday unless a beach is involved. And none more so than camping holidays. The archetypal sun, sea and sand holiday is, for some, the ideal; for others it's dramatic blustery seascapes and clattering, pebble beaches; yet others prefer secluded little coves and rocky inlets.

Whichever you prefer, this guide features campsites that offer all kinds of beach. There are even wonderful campsites set beside magnificent lakes, complete with their own beach.

So whether you're planning an out-of-season, invigorating seaside break or the full, sandy, bucket and spade extravaganza this summer, read on. There are 101 campsites in this guide and, depending on what kind of beach you're looking for, you are sure to find your ideal holiday destination here.

Alan Rogers – in search of 'the best'

Alan Rogers himself started off with the very specific aim of providing people with the necessary information to allow them to make an informed decision about their holiday destination. Today we still do that with a range of guides that now covers Europe's best campsites in 27 countries.

We work with campsites all day, every day. We visit campsites for inspection purposes (or even just for pleasure!). We know campsites 'inside out'.

We know which campsites would suit active families; which are great for get-away-from-it-all couples; we know which campsites are planning super new pool complexes; which campsites offer a fantastic menu in their on-site restaurant; which campsites allow you to launch a small boat from their slipway; which campsites have a decent playing area for kicking a ball around; which campsites have flat, grassy pitches and which have solid hard standings.

We also know which are good for fishing, golf, spas and outdoor activities; which are close to the beach; and which welcome dogs. These particular themes form our new '101' series.

All Alan Rogers guides (and our website) are respected for their independent, impartial and honest assessment. The reviews are prose-based, without overuse of indecipherable icons and symbols. Our simple aim is to help guide you to a campsite that matches best your requirements – often quite difficult in today's age of information overload.

What is the **best**?

The criteria we use when inspecting and selecting sites are numerous, but the most important by far is the question of good quality. People want different things from their choice of campsite, so campsite 'styles' vary dramatically: from small peaceful campsites in the heart of the countryside, to 'all singing, all dancing' sites in popular seaside resorts.

The size of the site, whether it's part of a chain or privately owned, makes no difference in terms of it being required to meet our exacting standards in respect of its quality and it being 'fit for purpose'. In other words, irrespective of the size of the site, or the number of facilities it offers, we consider and evaluate the welcome, the pitches, the sanitary facilities, the cleanliness, the general maintenance and even the location.

Expert opinions

We rely on our dedicated team of Site Assessors, all of whom are experienced campers, caravanners or motorcaravanners, to visit and recommend campsites. Each year they travel around Europe inspecting new campsites for Alan Rogers and re-inspecting the existing ones.

When planning
your **holiday...**

A holiday should always be a relaxing affair, and a campsite-based holiday particularly so. Our aim is for you to find the ideal campsite for your holiday, one that suits your requirements. All Alan Rogers guides provide a wealth of information, including some details supplied by campsite owners themselves, and the following points may help ensure that you plan a successful holiday.

Find out more

An Alan Rogers reference number (eg **FR 12345**) is given for each campsite and can be useful for finding more information and pictures online at **www.alanrogers.com**
Simply enter this number in the 'Campsite Search' field on the Home page.

Campsite descriptions

We aim to convey an idea of its general appearance, 'feel' and features, with details of pitch numbers, electricity, hardstandings etc.

Facilities

We list specific information on the site's facilities and amenities and, where available, the dates when these facilities are open (if not for the whole season). Much of this information is as supplied to us and may be subject to change. Should any particular activity or aspect of the campsite be important to you, it is always worth discussing with the campsite before you travel.

Swimming pools

Opening dates, any charges and levels of supervision are provided where we have been notified. In some countries (notably France) there is a regulation whereby Bermuda-style shorts may not be worn in swimming pools (for health and hygiene reasons). It is worth ensuring that you do take 'proper' swimming trunks with you.

Charges

Those given are the latest provided to us, usually 2010 prices, and should be viewed as a guide only.

Toilet blocks

We assume that toilet blocks will be equipped with a reasonable number of British style WCs, washbasins and hot showers in cubicles. We also assume that there will be an identified chemical toilet disposal point, and that the campsite will provide water and waste water drainage points and bin areas. If not the case, we comment. We do mention certain features that some readers find important: washbasins in cubicles, facilities for babies, facilities for those with disabilities and motorcaravan service points.

Reservations

Necessary for high season (roughly mid-July to mid-August) in popular holiday areas (i.e. beach resorts). You can reserve many sites via our own Alan Rogers Travel Service or through other tour operators. Remember, many sites are closed all winter and you may struggle to get an answer.

Telephone numbers

All numbers assume that you are phoning from within the country in question. From the UK or Ireland, dial 00, then the country's prefix (e.g. France is 33), then the campsite number given, but dropping the first '0'.

Opening dates

Dates given are those provided to us and can alter before the start of the season. If you intend to visit shortly after a published opening date, or shortly before the closing date, it is wise to check that it will actually be open at the time required. Similarly some sites operate a restricted service during the low season, only opening some of their facilities (e.g. swimming pools) during the main season; where we know about this, and have the relevant dates, we indicate it – again if you are at all doubtful it is wise to check.

Accommodation

Over recent years, more and more campsites have added high quality mobile homes, chalets, lodges, gites and more. Where applicable we indicate what is available and you'll find details online.

Special Offers

Some campsites have taken the opportunity to highlight a special offer. This is arranged by them and for clarification please contact the campsite direct.

Life's
a **beach**

The lure of the coast, and the beach in particular, is a strong holiday motivation. Most people enjoy a holiday beside the sea, and the many facets a beach has to offer holidaymakers of all ages. There are thousands of campsites across Europe, with many on or close to a great beach either on the coast or beside a shimmering lake. This guide features a short-list of just 101 so read on and start dreaming…

Why the beach...?

In the UK, it was not until the advent of the train in the late 19th century that the masses began to enjoy the benefits of a seaside holiday, fuelling growth of long piers. Later, from the 1920s, glamour became part of the mix, with the south of France attracting the likes of Hemingway and Picasso. An hotel was encouraged to stay open all summer and the Côte d'Azur has never looked back. Venerable fashionable resorts (Biarritz, La Baule) are still going strong; sandy expanses in the West Country are perennial favourites; the blustery Scandanavian beaches are atmospheric and unspoilt; and the vast sandy beaches of the Spanish Costas offer a special magic.

Finding the right **beach campsite**

Sun, sea and sand...it sounds simple but finding the right balance can be difficult with a campsite beach holiday. Some people want to be right there in the action, right on the beach; others prefer a campsite that's set back from the hurly-burly, even if it means a short drive. Some simply want miles of sand, with or without the crowds, others search for secluded rocky coves, perhaps seeking out that perfect spot beneath a shady pine.

You will find campsites with majestic sweeping sea views, campsites which run regular shuttle buses to and from the beach – especially handy when parking is at a premium; some campsites have their very own private stretch of beach and this may vary between sand, shingle, craggy rocks and dunes.

Quality Beaches

What makes a good beach? Which is the best beach in the area? Which beach is best for children? These are all valid questions but everyone will have their own opinion.

Blue Flag

Blue Flag is a prestigious international award scheme for beaches which acts as a guarantee of quality. Awarded annually to over 3,450 beaches and marinas in 41 countries, the award of a Blue Flag is based on compliance with 32 criteria covering the aspects of:

- Environmental Education and Information
- Water Quality
- Environmental Management
- Safety and Services

Children
on **beaches**

Family memories are made of long sunny days at the beach: splashing in the shallows, sandcastles, sandy sandwiches, buckets of crabs.

A good family beach, especially for young children, will have clean sand (ideally of the kind that makes good sandcastles), gently sloping down to the sea. Hopefully the sea at low tide is not a mile away, allowing toddlers to paddle while remaining close by (although a lovely wide beach does allow plenty of room for games and kite flying). And of course an ice cream vendor can usually bring a few squeals of pleasure!

Activities for children

Some larger beaches often have activities specially for children, usually in high season – these could range from playgrounds or boating lakes right up to paid-for clubs with organised activities all day. And of course, in the UK the traditional donkey ride still exists!

For the younger ones

- Dig a channel to the sea
- Make a dam
- Bury dad in the sand
- Go beach combing for the most interesting "find"
- Build a boat or a car in the sand big enough to sit in – always makes an amusing snap for the album!

Ping Pong Ball Race

Dig a series of sloping channels wide enough (and smooth enough) to take a ping pong ball. Place ping pong balls at the start line and then race each other, blowing the ball down the channel to the finish line.

Beach Mini Golf

Create your own mini golf course in the sand. Players take turns with a plastic golf club and ball - or whatever implement you can find.

Frisbee

A perennial favourite. Set up some targets in the sand and see who can get closest, or arrange plastic bottles in the sand and try to knock them over.

Go prepared and keep a bat and ball in the car – there's always a demand for French cricket, boules, badminton and kite flying.

Water Fun

Many lakeside campsites, especially in Austria, Hungary and Slovenia, have pedaloes, row boats and floating pontoons, as well as on-shore activities.

on the **beach**

With a bracing breeze, a good boost of ozone and loads of space, a beach always seems to invite activity. It could be a fairly sedate activity like beach combing, throwing the odd stick for a dog or flying a kite. Fishing too is popular, available all year, and for free.

More strenuous and physical activities might include power kiting and sand yachting – popular on the longest, wide flat sandy beaches.

Surfing

By definition, good surfing beaches will involve turbulent waters so try and surf where a lifeguard is present and not on your own. Only surf within your own ability and experience, making sure you are surfing in safe locations.

Kayaking

A great way to spend time on the water but don't take this too lightly – you should be familiar with the necessary kit and precautions. Check the weather, wind and tides, wear a buoyancy aid and ideally paddle in a group, telling someone back on land where you are going. Make sure you can get back on board your kayak should you capsize.

Staying safe
at the beach

Beaches are a fun environment but it pays to be aware of potential dangers. In particular, keep an eye on tides – incoming tides can quickly trap people in coves or under cliffs. If unsure, check with a lifeguard. The RNLI beach safety tips are applicable anywhere.

Top Tips

- Always swim at a lifeguarded beach

- Swim between the red and yellow flags *(UK)*

- Never swim alone

- Never use inflatables in strong winds or rough seas

- If you get into trouble, wave and call for help

- If you see someone else in trouble, tell a lifeguard or call emergency services

- Take note of warnings and notices

Enjoy…!

Whether you're an 'old hand' or are contemplating your first trip, a regular reader of our Guides or a new 'convert', we wish you well in your travels and hope we have been able to help in some way. We are, of course, also out and about ourselves, visiting sites, talking to owners and readers, and generally checking on standards and new developments. We hope to bump into you!

Wishing you thoroughly enjoyable camping and caravanning in 2011 – favoured by good weather of course!

The Alan Rogers Team

Further **information**

www.goodbeachguide.co.uk
Website of the Marine Conservation Society

www.blueflag.org
*The international organisation responsible for awarding
the Blue Flag for beaches (and marinas)*

www.onbeach.nl
Dutch website with information and lists of European beaches

www.maplage.fr
French website with extensive information on French beaches

www.esplaya.com
English-language website on the many beaches in Spain

www.italyheaven.co.uk
English-language website on the beaches of Italy

www.kustgids.nl and www.holland.com
*Respectively, a Dutch and an English-language website
on the beaches of the Netherlands*

Camping La Gaviota

Ctra de la Platja s/n, E-17470 Sant Pere Pescador (Girona)
t: 972 520 569 e: info@lagaviota.com
alanrogers.com/ES80310 www.lagaviota.com

Accommodation: ☑ Pitch ☑ Mobile home/chalet ☐ Hotel/B&B ☐ Apartment

La Gaviota is a delightful, small, family run site at the end of a cul-de-sac with direct beach access. This ensures a peaceful situation with a choice of the pleasant L-shaped pool or direct beach access to the fine clean beach and slowly shelving access to the water. Everything here is clean and smart and the Gil family are very keen that you enjoy your time here. There are 165 touring pitches on flat ground with shade and electricity supply (6A). A lush green feel is given to the site by many palms and other semi-tropical trees and shrubs. The restaurant and bar are very pleasant indeed and have a distinct Spanish flavour. The cuisine is reasonably priced, perfectly prepared and served by friendly staff. All facilities are at the reception end of this rectangular site with extra washing up areas at the far end. The guests here were happy and enjoying themselves when we visited. English is spoken.

You might like to know

This is one of the most important protected natural areas of Catalonia, because it brings together rare specimen of flora and fauna, and also is a stepping stone and a refuge for thousands of migratory birds.

☑ Beach on site
☐ Beach within 1 km.
☑ Sandy beach
☐ Blue Flag quality
☐ Lifeguard (high season)
☐ Sun lounger/deckchair hire
☑ Watersports
   (e.g. sailing, windsurfing)
☑ Snacks and drinks
☐ Sunshades
☐ Dogs allowed (on the beach)

Facilities: One smart and very clean toilet block is near reception. All WCs are British style and the showers are excellent. Superb facilities for disabled visitors. Two great family rooms plus two baby rooms. Washing machine. Gas supplies. Supermarket (fresh bread). Pleasant bar and small, delightful restaurant. Swimming pool. Playground. Games room. Limited animation. Beach sports and windsurfing. Internet. Torches useful. ATM. Off site: Boat launching 2 km. Riding 4 km. Golf 15 km. Boat excursions. Cycling routes.

Open: 19 March - 24 October.

Directions: From the AP7/E15 take exit 3 onto the N11 north towards Figueras and then the C260 towards Roses. At Castello d'Empúries take the GIV 6216 and continue to Sant Pere Pescador. Site is well signed in the town. GPS: 42.18901, 3.10843

Charges guide

Per unit incl. 2 persons and electricity	€ 22,30 - € 50,70
extra person	€ 2,70 - € 3,90
child (under 10 yrs)	€ 1,40 - € 2,70
dog	€ 2,00 - € 4,00

No credit cards. Discounts for longer stays.

Camping Las Palmeras

Ctra de la Platja, E-17470 Sant Pere Pescador (Girona)
t: 972 520 506 e: info@campinglaspalmeras.com
alanrogers.com/ES80330 www.campinglaspalmeras.com

Accommodation: ☑Pitch ☑Mobile home/chalet ☐Hotel/B&B ☐Apartment

A very polished site, the pleasant experience begins as you enter the palm bedecked site and are greeted at the air conditioned reception building. The 230 pitches are flat, very clean and well maintained, with some shade and 10A electricity. A few pitches are complete with water and drainage. Thirty smart mobile homes are placed unobtrusively around the site. A very pleasant pool complex has a lifeguard and the brightly coloured play areas are clean and safe. The very pleasant beach is a 200 m. walk through a gate at the rear of the site. A full activities programme allows parents a break during the day and there is organised fun in the evenings in high season. The owner, Juan Carlos Alcantara, and his wife have many years experience in the campsite business which is clearly demonstrated. You will enjoy a stay here as there is a very happy atmosphere.

You might like to know
Las Palmeras is close to a large natural park, ideal for walking or cycling.

☐ Beach on site

☑ Beach within 1 km.

☑ Sandy beach

☑ Blue Flag quality

☑ Lifeguard *(high season)*

☐ Sun lounger/deckchair hire

☑ Watersports
  (e.g. sailing, windsurfing)

☑ Snacks and drinks

☑ Sunshades

☐ Dogs allowed *(on the beach)*

Facilities: Two excellent, very clean toilet blocks include first class facilities for disabled campers. Baby rooms. Facilities may become a little busy at peak periods. Washing machines. Motorcaravan services. Supermarket. Restaurant/bar (children's menu). Swimming pools (heated). Play areas. Tennis. Gym. Barbecue. Bicycle hire. Miniclub. Entertainment. Satellite TV. Internet access. ATM. Torches useful. Off site: Beach and fishing 200 m. Sailing and boat launching 2 km. Riding 4 km. Golf 7 km.

Open: 27 March - 23 October.

Directions: Sant Pere Pescador is south of Perpignan on coast between Roses and L'Escala. From the AP7/E15 take exit 4 onto the N11 north towards Figueres and then C31 towards Torroella de Fluvia. Take the Vilamacolum road east and continue to Sant Pere Pescador. Site well signed in town. GPS: 42.18805, 3.1027

Charges guide

Per unit incl. 2 persons and electricity	€ 21,70 - € 47,90
extra person	€ 2,50 - € 4,00
child (2-10 yrs)	€ 2,30
animal	€ 2,50 - € 4,00

SPAIN – Sant Pere Pescador

Kawan Village L'Amfora

2 avenida Josep Tarradellas, E-17470 Sant Pere Pescador (Girona)
t: 972 520 540 e: info@campingamfora.com
alanrogers.com/ES80350 www.campingamfora.com

Accommodation: ☑Pitch ☑Mobile home/chalet ☐Hotel/B&B ☑Apartment

This super, spacious site is family run and friendly. A Greek theme is manifested mainly in the restaurant and around the pool areas. The site is spotlessly clean and well maintained and the owner operates in an environmentally friendly way. There are 830 level, grass pitches (730 for touring units) laid out in a grid system, all with 10A electricity. Attractive trees and shrubs have been planted around each pitch. There is good shade in the more mature areas and these pitches include 64 large pitches (180 m²), each with an individual sanitary unit (toilet, shower and washbasin). The newer area is more open with less shade and you can choose which you would prefer. At the entrance a terraced bar and two restaurants overlook a smart pool complex that includes three pools for children, one with two water slides. In high season there is ambitious entertainment (pub, disco, shows) and an activity programme for children. Alongside the site, the magnificent sandy beach on the Bay of Roses offers good conditions for children and a choice of high season watersport activities.

Special offers
Low season offers for Senior Citizens (pitch):
10=9 (stay for 10 days, pay for 9)
or 14=12 / 18=14 / 22=15.
Low season accommodation offers:
7=5 14=10.

You might like to know
Sailing boats and catamarans can be hired on the beach.

☑ Beach on site
☐ Beach within 1 km.

☑ Sandy beach
☑ Blue Flag quality
☑ Lifeguard *(high season)*
☐ Sun lounger/deckchair hire
☑ Watersports
  (e.g. sailing, windsurfing)
☑ Snacks and drinks
☐ Sunshades
☑ Dogs allowed *(on the beach)*

Facilities: Three main toilet blocks, one heated, provide washbasins in cabins and roomy free showers. Baby rooms. Laundry facilities and laundry service. Motorcaravan services. Supermarket. Terraced bar, self-service and waiter service restaurants. Pizzeria/takeaway. Restaurant and bar on the beach with limited menu (high season). Disco bar. Swimming pools (1/5-30/9). Pétanque. Tennis. Bicycle hire. Minigolf. Play area. Miniclub. Entertainment and activities. Windsurfing. Boat launching and sailing. Fishing. Games and TV rooms. Internet room and WiFi. Off site: Riding 4 km. Golf 15 km.

Open: 29 March - 30 September.

Directions: From the north on A17/E15 take exit 3 onto N11 towards Figueres and then shortly onto the C260 towards Roses. At Castello d'Empúries turn right onto the GIV-6216 to Sant Pere. From the south on the A17 use exit 5 (L'Escala) and turn to Sant Pere in Viladamat. Site is well signed in the town towards the beach. GPS: 42.18147, 3.10405

Charges guide

Per person	€ 3,70 - € 5,00
child (2-9 yrs)	free - € 4,00
pitch (100 m²)	€ 16,00 - € 41,00

No credit cards.

Camping Las Dunas

Ctra San Marti - Sant Pere, E-17470 Sant Pere Pescador (Girona)
t: 972 521 717 e: info@campinglasdunas.com
alanrogers.com/ES80400 www.campinglasdunas.com

Accommodation: ☑Pitch ☑Mobile home/chalet ☐ Hotel/B&B ☐ Apartment

Las Dunas is an extremely large, impressive and well organised resort style site with many on-site activities and an ongoing programme of improvements. It has direct access to a superb sandy beach that stretches along the site for nearly a kilometre with a windsurfing school and beach bar. There is also a much used, huge swimming pool, plus a large double pool for children. Las Dunas is very large, with 1,700 individual hedged pitches (1,479 for tourers) of around 100 m². laid out on flat ground in long, regular parallel rows. All have electricity and 180 also have water and drainage. Shade is available in some parts of the site. Much effort has gone into planting palms and new trees here and the results are very attractive. The large restaurant and bar have spacious terraces overlooking the pools and you can enjoy a very pleasant, more secluded, cavern style pub. A magnificent disco club is close by in a soundproof building. With free quality entertainment of all types in season and positive security arrangements, this is a great site for families with teenagers. Member of Leading Campings Group.

You might like to know

Also on offer are all types of adventure sports including canoeing, hot air balloon excursions, monoplane flights and gliding.

- ☑ **Beach on site**
- ☐ **Beach within 1 km.**
- ☑ **Sandy beach**
- ☑ **Blue Flag quality**
- ☑ **Lifeguard** *(high season)*
- ☐ **Sun lounger/deckchair hire**
- ☑ **Watersports** *(e.g. sailing, windsurfing)*
- ☑ **Snacks and drinks**
- ☐ **Sunshades**
- ☐ **Dogs allowed** *(on the beach)*

Facilities: Five excellent large toilet blocks with electronic sliding glass doors (resident cleaners 07.00-21.00). Excellent facilities for youngsters, babies and disabled people. Laundry facilities. Motorcaravan services. Extensive supermarket, boutique and other shops. Large bar with terrace. Large restaurant. Takeaway. Ice cream parlour. Beach bar in main season. Disco club. Swimming pools. Playgrounds. Tennis. Archery. Minigolf. Sailing/windsurfing school and other watersports. Programme of sports, games, excursions and entertainment, partly in English (15/6-31/8). ATM. Safety deposit. Internet café. WiFi. Off site: Riding and boat launching 5 km. Water park 10 km. Golf 30 km. L'Escala 5 km.

Open: 19 May - 2 September.

Directions: L'Escala is northeast of Girona on the coast between Palamós and Roses. From A7/E15 autostrada take exit 5 towards L'Escala on GI 623. Turn north 2 km. before reaching L'Escala towards Sant Marti d'Ampúrias. Site is well signed. GPS: 42.16098, 3.13478

Charges guide

Per person	€ 3,50 - € 5,00
child (2-10 yrs)	€ 3,00 - € 3,25
pitch	€ 14,00 - € 52,00
dog	€ 3,20 - € 4,50

SPAIN – Sant Pere Pescador

Camping Aquarius

Playa s/n, E-17470 Sant Pere Pescador (Girona)
t: 972 520 003   e: camping@aquarius.es
alanrogers.com/ES80500   www.aquarius.es

Accommodation: ☑Pitch ☑Mobile home/chalet ☐ Hotel/B&B ☐ Apartment

A smart and efficient family site, Aquarius has direct access to a quiet sandy beach that slopes gently and provides good bathing (the sea is shallow for quite a long way out). Watersports are popular, particularly windsurfing (a school is provided). One third of the site has good shade with a park-like atmosphere. There are 435 pitches with electricity (6/16A). Markus Rupp and his wife are keen to make every visitor's experience a happy one. The site is ideal for those who really like sun and sea, with a quiet situation. The family is justifiably proud of their most attractive and absolutely pristine site which they continually upgrade and improve. The fountain at the entrance, the fishponds and the water features in the restaurant are soothing and pleasing. A small stage close to the restaurant is used for live entertainment in season. The spotless beach bar complex with shaded terraces, satellite TV and evening entertainment, has marvellous views over the Bay of Roses. The Surf Centre with rentals, school and shop is ideal for enthusiasts and beginners alike.

You might like to know

The broad, 10 kilometre long, sandy beach is one of the last beaches remaining in its natural state on this coast. The sea is clear and shallow, ideal for children.

☑ Beach on site
☐ Beach within 1 km.

☑ Sandy beach
☑ Blue Flag quality
☐ Lifeguard *(high season)*
☐ Sun lounger/deckchair hire
☑ Watersports
   (e.g. sailing, windsurfing)
☑ Snacks and drinks
☐ Sunshades
☑ Dogs allowed *(on the beach)*

Facilities: Attractively tiled, fully equipped, large toilet blocks provide some cabins for each sex. Excellent facilities for disabled people, plus baths for children. Superb new block has underfloor heating and family cabins. Laundry. Gas supplies. Motorcaravan services. Full size refrigerators. Supermarket. Pleasant restaurant and bar with terrace. Takeaway. Purpose built play centre for children (with qualified attendant), playground and separate play area for toddlers. TV room. Surf Centre. Minigolf. Bicycle hire. ATM. Internet access. WiFi. Dogs are accepted in one section. (Note: no pool). Off site: Fishing and boat launching 3 km. Riding 6 km. Golf 15 km.

Open: 15 March - 31 October.

Directions: Sant Pere Pescador is on the coast between Roses and L'Escala. From the AP7/E15 take exit 4 onto the N11 north towards Figueras and then the C31 towards Torroella de Fluvia. Take the Vilamacolum road east and continue to Sant Pere . Site well signed in town. GPS: 42.1769, 3.10797

Charges guide

Per person	€ 3,00 - € 4,00
child (under 12 yrs)	free - € 2,65
pitch incl. electricity	€ 8,80 - € 44,50

No credit cards.

Camping La Ballena Alegre

E-17470 Sant Pere Pescador (Girona)
t: 902 510 520   e: infb2@ballena-alegre.com
alanrogers.com/ES80600   www.ballena-alegre.com

Accommodation: ☑Pitch ☑Mobile home/chalet ☐ Hotel/B&B ☐ Apartment

La Ballena Alegre is partly in a lightly wooded setting, partly open, and has almost 2 km. of frontage directly onto an excellent beach of soft golden sand (which is cleaned daily). They claim that none of the 1,531 touring pitches is more than 100 m. from the beach. The grass pitches are numbered and there is a choice of size (up to 100 m²). Electrical connections (5/10A) are available in all areas and there are 378 fully serviced pitches. A recent addition is a resort village area within the site with holiday homes and its own small pool and play area. This is a great site for families. There are restaurant and bar areas beside the pleasant terraced pool complex (four pools including a pool for children). For those who wish to drink and snack late there is a pub open until 03.00. The well managed, soundproofed disco is popular with youngsters. A little train ferries people along the length of the site and a road train runs to local villages. Plenty of entertainment and activities are offered, including a well managed watersports centre, with subaqua, windsurfing and kite surfing.

You might like to know
You will find the ideal spot to spend a good time with your family. The campsite is situated along a 1,800 m. long, large and sandy beach. The campsite boasts Club Mistral, a specialist wind and kite surf school.

☑ Beach on site
☐ Beach within 1 km.
☑ Sandy beach
☐ Blue Flag quality
☑ Lifeguard *(high season)*
☐ Sun lounger/deckchair hire
☑ Watersports
    (e.g. sailing, windsurfing)
☑ Snacks and drinks
☐ Sunshades
☑ Dogs allowed *(on the beach)*

Facilities: Seven well maintained toilet blocks are of a very high standard. Facilities for children, babies and disabled campers. Launderette. Motorcaravan services. Gas supplies. Supermarket. 'Linen' restaurant. Self-service restaurant and bar. Takeaway. Pizzeria and beach bar in high season. Swimming pool complex. Jacuzzi. Tennis. Watersports centre. Fitness centre. Bicycle hire. Playgrounds. Sound proofed disco. Dancing twice weekly and organised activities, sports, entertainment, etc. ATM. Internet access and WiFi. Torches useful in beach areas. Off site: Go-karting nearby with bus service. Fishing 300 m. Riding 2 km.

Open: 14 May - 20 September.

Directions: From A7 Figueres - Girona autopista take exit 5 to L'Escala GI 623 for 18.5 km. At roundabout take sign to Sant Marti d'Empúries and follow site signs. GPS: 42.15323, 3.11248

Charges guide

Per unit incl. 2 persons and electricity	€ 25,00 - € 70,00
extra person	€ 3,75 - € 4,54
child (3-9 yrs)	€ 2,70 - € 3,28
dog	€ 2,25 - € 4,74

Discount of 10% on pitch charge for pensioners all season. No credit cards.

SPAIN – Calonge

Camping Internacional de Calonge

Ctra San Feliu/Guixols - Palamós, E-17251 Calonge (Girona)
t: 972 651 233   e: info@intercalonge.com
alanrogers.com/ES81300   www.intercalonge.com

Accommodation: ☑Pitch ☑Mobile home/chalet ☐Hotel/B&B ☐Apartment

This spacious, well laid out site has access to a fine beach by a footbridge over the coast road, or you can take the little road train as the site is on very sloping ground. Calonge is a family site with two good sized pools on different levels, a paddling pool, plus large sunbathing areas. A great new restaurant, bar and snack bar are by the pool. The site's 793 pitches are on terraces and all have electricity (5A), with 84 being fully serviced. The pitches are set on attractively landscaped terraces (access to some may be challenging). There is good shade from the tall pine trees and some views of the sea through the foliage. The views from the upper levels are taken by the tour operator and mobile home pitches. The pools are overlooked by the restaurant terraces which have great views over the mountains. A separate area within the site is set aside for visitors with dogs (including a dog shower!) The beach is accessed via 100 steps and is shared with another campsite.

Special offers
For this year's offers contact the campsite.

You might like to know
Visit magical cities like Barcelona, Girona or Figueres where you can choose from a vast range of cultural, sporting and leisure activities.

☐ Beach on site
☑ Beach within 1 km.

☑ Sandy beach
☑ Blue Flag quality
☑ Lifeguard *(high season)*
☐ Sun lounger/deckchair hire
☑ Watersports
   (e.g. sailing, windsurfing)
☑ Snacks and drinks
☑ Sunshades
☐ Dogs allowed *(on the beach)*

Facilities: Generous sanitary provision in new or renovated blocks include some washbasins in cabins. No toilet seats. One block is heated in winter. Laundry facilities. Motorcaravan services. Gas supplies. Shop (27/3-31/10), Bar/restaurant, Patio bar (pizza and takeaway) all 27/3-24/10, weekends for the rest of the year. Swimming pools (27/3-12/10). Playground. Electronic games. Rather noisy disco two nights a week (but not late). Bicycle hire. Tennis. Hairdresser. ATM. Internet access and WiFi. Road train from the bottom of the site to the top in high season. Off site: Bus at the gate. Fishing 300 m. Supermarket 500 m. Golf 3 km. Riding 10 km.

Open: All year.

Directions: Site is on the inland side of the coast road between Palamós and Platja d'Aro. Take the C31 south to the 661 at Calonge. At Calonge follow signs to the C253 towards Platja d'Aro and on to the site. GPS: 41.83333, 3.08417

Charges guide

Per unit incl. 2 persons

and electricity	€ 19,65 - € 44,65
extra person	€ 3,65 - € 7,85
child (3-10 yrs)	€ 1,85 - € 4,40
dog	€ 3,20 - € 4,05

No credit cards.

SPAIN – Tossa de Mar

Camping Cala Llevadó

Ctra GI-682 de Tossa a Lloret pk. 18,9, E-17320 Tossa de Mar (Girona)
t: 972 340 314 e: info@calallevado.com
alanrogers.com/ES82000 www.calallevado.com

Accommodation: ☑Pitch ☑Mobile home/chalet ☐ Hotel/B&B ☐ Apartment

For splendour of position, Cala Llevadó can compare with almost any in this guide. A beautifully situated cliff-side site, enjoying fine views of the sea and coast below. It is shaped something like half a bowl with steep slopes. High up in the site with a superb aspect, is the attractive restaurant/bar with a large terrace overlooking the pleasant swimming pool directly below. There are terraced, flat areas for caravans and tents (with 10/16A electricity) on the upper levels of the two slopes, with a great many individual pitches for tents scattered around the site. Some of these pitches have fantastic settings and views. Many of the 577 touring pitches are available for caravans. The steepness of the site would make access difficult for disabled people or those with limited mobility. One beach is for all manner of watersports within a buoyed area and there is a subaqua diving school. Some other pleasant little coves can also be reached by climbing down on foot (with care!). Cala Llevadó is luxurious and has much character and the atmosphere is informal and very friendly.

Special offers
Special rates at the Diving Centre.

You might like to know
Very beautiful beaches within easy reach; one of the most scenic parts of the Costa Brava.

☑ **Beach on site**
☐ Beach within 1 km.

☑ **Sandy beach**
☐ Blue Flag quality
☐ **Lifeguard** (high season)
☐ Sun lounger/deckchair hire
☑ **Watersports**
   (e.g. sailing, windsurfing)
☑ **Snacks and drinks**
☐ **Sunshades**
☐ **Dogs allowed** (on the beach)

Facilities: Four very well equipped toilet blocks are immaculately maintained and well spaced around the site. Baby baths. Laundry facilities. Motorcaravan services. Gas supplies. Fridge hire. Large supermarket. Restaurant/bar (5/5-28/9). Swimming and paddling pools. Three play areas. Botanic garden. Entertainment for children (4-12 yrs). Sailing, water skiing and windsurfing school. Fishing. Excursions. Internet access and WiFi. Torches definitely needed in some areas. Off site: Bicycle hire 3 km. Riding 10 km. Large complex adjacent for sports, activities and swimming.

Open: 1 May - 30 September.

Directions: Cala Llevadó is southeast of Girona on the coast. Leave the AP7/E15 at exit 7 to the C65 Sant Feliu road and then take the C35 southeast to the GI 681 to Tossa de Mar. Site is signed off the GI 682 Lloret - Tossa road at km. 18,9, about 3 km. from Tossa. Route avoids difficult coastal road. GPS: 41.71282, 2.90623

Charges guide

Per unit incl. 2 persons and electricity	€ 29,00 - € 49,30
extra person	€ 5,80 - € 9,75
child (4-12 yrs)	€ 3,35 - € 5,20

Camping & Bungalows Sanguli

Prolongacion Calle, Apdo 123, E-43840 Salou (Tarragona)
t: 977 381 641   e: mail@sanguli.es
alanrogers.com/ES84800   www.sanguli.es

Accommodation: ☑Pitch ☑Mobile home/chalet ☐ Hotel/B&B ☐ Apartment

Sanguli is a superb site boasting excellent pools and ambitious entertainment. Owned, developed and managed by a local Spanish family, it provides for all the family with everything open when the site is open. There are 1,067 pitches of varying size (75-90 m²) and all have electricity. About 100 are used by tour operators and 207 for bungalows. A wonderful selection of trees, palms and shrubs provides natural shade. The good sandy beach is little more than 100 metres across the coast road and a small railway crossing (a little noise). Although large, Sanguli has a pleasant, open feel and maintains a quality family atmosphere due to the efforts of the very keen and efficient staff. There are three very attractive pool areas, one (heated) near the entrance with a grassy sunbathing area partly shaded and a second deep one with water slides that forms part of the excellent sports complex (with fitness centre, tennis courts, minigolf and football practice area). This is a large, professional site providing something for all the family, but still capable of providing peace and quiet for those looking for it.

You might like to know

Activities on the beach include windsurfing, sailing, waterskiing, pedaloes and, 800 m. from here, sea fishing. The attractive seafront promenade will take you into the centre of Salou.

☐ **Beach on site**
☑ **Beach within 1 km.**
☑ **Sandy beach**
☐ **Blue Flag quality**
☐ **Lifeguard** (high season)
☐ **Sun lounger/deckchair hire**
☑ **Watersports**
  (e.g. sailing, windsurfing)
☐ **Snacks and drinks**
☐ **Sunshades**
☐ **Dogs allowed** (on the beach)

Facilities: The six quality sanitary facilities are constantly cleaned and are always exceptional, including many individual cabins with en-suite facilities. Improvements are made each year. Some blocks have excellent facilities for babies. Launderette with service. Motorcaravan services. Car wash (charged). Bars and restaurant with takeaway. Swimming pools. Jacuzzi. Fitness centre. Sports complex. Fitness room (charged). Playgrounds. Miniclub, teenagers club. Internet room. Upmarket minigolf. First-aid room. Gas supplies. Multiple internet options including WiFi. Security bracelets for children under 12 years. Off site: Bus at gate. Fishing and bicycle hire 100 m. Riding 3 km. Golf 6 km.

Open: 19 March - 1 November.

Directions: On west side of Salou about 1 km. from the centre, site is well signed from the coast road to Cambrils and from the other town approaches. GPS: 41.075, 1.116

Charges guide

Per person	€ 6,00
child (4-12 yrs)	€ 4,00
pitch incl. electricity	€ 15,00 - € 52,00
incl. water and drainage	€ 17,00 - € 55,00

Camping-Pension Cala d'Oques

Via Augusta s/n, E-43890 Hospitalet del Infante (Tarragona)
t: 977 823 254 e: eroller@tinet.org
alanrogers.com/ES85350 www.caladoques.com

Accommodation: ☑Pitch ☑Mobile home/chalet ☑Hotel/B&B ☐ Apartment

This peaceful and delightful site has been developed with care and dedication by Elisa Roller over 40 years or so and she now runs it with the help of her daughter Kim. Part of its appeal lies in its situation beside the sea with a wide beach of sand and pebbles, its amazing mountain backdrop and the views across the bay to the town and part by the atmosphere created by Elisa and her staff – friendly, relaxed and comfortable. There are 255 pitches, mostly level and laid out beside the beach, with more behind on wide, informal terracing. Electricity is available although long leads may be needed in places. Pine and olive trees are an attractive feature and provide some shade. The restaurant with its homely touches has a super menu and a reputation extending well outside the site, and the family type entertainment is in total contrast to that provided at the larger, brasher sites of the Costa Daurada. Gates provide access to the pleasant beach with useful cold showers to wash the sand away. Torches are needed at night. This is a pretty place to stay and Elisa gives a pleasant personal service.

Special offers
Low Season discounts:
2 days = 5% discount
4 days = 10% discount
7 days = 15% discount
14 days = 20% discount

You might like to know
The campsite is located right on the beach and is open all year. There is generally no need to reserve.

☑ Beach on site
☐ Beach within 1 km.

☑ Sandy beach
☑ Blue Flag quality
☑ Lifeguard *(high season)*
☐ Sun lounger/deckchair hire
☑ Watersports
  (e.g. sailing, windsurfing)
☑ Snacks and drinks
☐ Sunshades
☑ Dogs allowed *(on the beach)*

Facilities: Toilet facilities are in the front part of the main building. Clean and neat, there is hot water to showers (hot water by token but free to campers – to guard against unauthorised visitors from the beach). New heated unit with toilets and washbasins for winter use. Additional small block with toilets and washbasins at the far end of the site. Motorcaravan service point. Restaurant/bar and shop (1/4-30/10). Play area. Kim's kids club. Fishing. Internet access and WiFi. Gas supplies. Off site: Village facilities, incl. shop and restaurant 1.5 km. Bicycle hire and riding 2 km.

Open: All year.

Directions: Hospitalet del Infante is south of Tarragona, accessed from the A7 (exit 38) or from the N340. From the north take first exit to Hospitalet del Infante at the 1128 km. marker. Follow signs in the village, site is 2 km. south, by the sea. GPS: 40.97777, 0.90338

Charges guide

Per unit incl. 2 persons and electricity	€ 21,15 - € 36,75
extra person	€ 4,95 - € 9,30
child (0-10 yrs)	€ 1,50
dog	€ 3,30

Discounts for seniors and for longer stays. No credit cards.

Camping Roche

N340 km 19,5, Carril de Pilahito, E-11140 Conil de la Frontera (Cádiz)
t: 956 442 216   e: info@campingroche.com
alanrogers.com/ES88590   www.campingroche.com

Accommodation: ☑Pitch ☑Mobile home/chalet ☐ Hotel/B&B ☐ Apartment

Camping Roche is situated in a pine forest near white sandy beaches in the lovely region of Andalucia. It is a clean and tidy, welcoming site. Little English is spoken but try your Spanish, German or French as the staff are very helpful. A family site, it offers a variety of facilities including a sports area and swimming pools. The restaurant has good food and a pleasant outlook over the pool. Games are organised for children. A recently built extension provides further pitches, a new toilet block and a tennis court. There are now 335 pitches which include 104 bungalows to rent. There are pleasant paths in the area for mountain biking.

You might like to know

The campsite is well situated for visiting the wonderful cities of Seville and Cadiz.

☐ Beach on site
☑ Beach within 1 km.

☑ Sandy beach
☐ Blue Flag quality
☐ Lifeguard *(high season)*
☐ Sun lounger/deckchair hire
☑ Watersports
   (e.g. sailing, windsurfing)
☑ Snacks and drinks
☐ Sunshades
☐ Dogs allowed *(on the beach)*

Facilities: Three toilet blocks are traditional in style and provide simple, clean facilities. Washbasins have cold water only. Washing machine. Supermarket. Bar and restaurant. Swimming and paddling pools. Sports area. Tennis. Play area. Off site: Bus stops 3 times daily outside gates.

Open: All year.

Directions: From the N340 (Cádiz - Algeciras) turn off to site at km. 19.5 point. From Conil, take El Pradillo road. Keep following signs to the site. From CA3208 road turn at km. 1 and site is 1.5 km. down this road on the right.
GPS: 36.31089, -6.11268

Charges guide

Per unit incl. 2 persons and electricity	€ 33,00
extra person	€ 6,50
child	€ 5,50
dog	€ 3,75

Low season discounts.

Camping Marjal

Ctra N332 km 73,4, E-03140 Guardamar del Segura (Alacant)
t: 966 727 070   e: camping@marjal.com
alanrogers.com/ES87430   www.campingmarjal.com

Accommodation: ☑ Pitch ☑ Mobile home/chalet   ☐ Hotel/B&B ☐ Apartment

Marjal is located beside the estuary of the Segura river, alongside the pine and eucalyptus forests of the Dunas de Guardamar natural park. The fine sandy beach can be reached through the forest (800 m). This is a new site with a huge lagoon-style pool and a superb sports complex. There are 212 pitches on this award winning site, all with water, electricity, drainage and satellite TV points. The ground is covered with crushed marble, making the pitches clean and pleasant. There is some shade and the site has an open feel with lots of room for manoeuvring. The impressive pool/lagoon complex (1,100 m²) has a water cascade, an island bar plus bridge, one part sectioned as a pool for children and a jacuzzi. The extensive sports area is also impressive with qualified instructors. No effort has been spared here; the quality heated indoor pool, light-exercise room, sauna, solarium, beauty salon, fully equipped gym with changing rooms, with facilities for disabled visitors, are of the highest quality. Aerobics and physiotherapy are also on offer.

You might like to know

Why not take a day trip to Guardamar del Segura, a typical Spanish town which has excellent beaches, a thriving street market and a variety of shops, bars and restaurants.

☐ **Beach on site**

☑ **Beach within 1 km.**

☑ **Sandy beach**

☑ **Blue Flag quality**

☐ **Lifeguard** *(high season)*

☐ **Sun lounger/deckchair hire**

☑ **Watersports**
(e.g. sailing, windsurfing)

☐ **Snacks and drinks**

☐ **Sunshades**

☐ **Dogs allowed** *(on the beach)*

Facilities: Three excellent heated toilet blocks have free hot water, elegant separators between sinks, spacious showers and some cabins. Each block has high quality facilities for babies and disabled campers, modern laundry and dishwashing rooms. Car wash. Well stocked supermarket. Restaurants. Bar. Large outdoor pool complex (1/6-31/10). Heated indoor pool (low season). Fitness suite. Jacuzzi. Sauna. Solarium. Aerobics and aquarobics. Play room. Minigolf. Floodlit tennis and soccer pitch. Bicycle hire. Games room. TV room. ATM. Business centre. Internet access. Off site: Beach 800 m. Riding and golf 4 km.

Open: All year.

Directions: On N332 40 km. south of Alicante, site is on the sea side between 73 and 74 km. markers. GPS: 38.10933, -0.65467

Charges guide

Per unit incl. 2 persons and electricity	€ 38,00 - € 63,00
extra person	€ 7,00 - € 9,00
child (4-12 yrs)	€ 5,00 - € 6,00
dog	€ 2,20 - € 3,20

Camping Playa Joyel

Playa de Ris, E-39180 Noja (Cantabria)
t: **942 630 081**   e: **playajoyel@telefonica.net**
alanrogers.com/ES90000   www.playajoyel.com

Accommodation: ☑Pitch ☑Mobile home/chalet ☐Hotel/B&B ☐Apartment

This very attractive holiday and touring site is some 40 kilometres from Santander and 80 kilometres from Bilbao. It is a busy, high quality, comprehensively equipped site by a superb beach providing 1,000 well shaded, marked and numbered pitches with 6A electricity available. These include 80 large pitches of 100 m². Some 250 pitches are occupied by tour operators or seasonal units. This well managed site has a lot to offer for family holidays with much going on in high season when it gets crowded. The swimming pool complex (with lifeguard) is free to campers and the superb beaches are cleaned daily 15/6-20/9. Two beach exits lead to the main beach where there are some undertows, or if you turn left you will find a reasonably placid estuary. An unusual feature here is the natural park within the site boundary which has a selection of animals to see. This overlooks a protected area of marsh where European birds spend the winter.

You might like to know

The fine sandy beach, which is excellent for surfing, is cleaned daily. Low tide reveals warm pools for younger children and rock pools with small fish and crabs.

☑ **Beach on site**
☐ **Beach within 1 km.**

☑ **Sandy beach**
☐ **Blue Flag quality**
☐ **Lifeguard** *(high season)*
☐ **Sun lounger/deckchair hire**
☑ **Watersports**
   (e.g. sailing, windsurfing)
☐ **Snacks and drinks**
☐ **Sunshades**
☐ **Dogs allowed** *(on the beach)*

Facilities: Six excellent, spacious and fully equipped toilet blocks include baby baths. Large laundry. Motorcaravan services. Gas supplies. Freezer service. Supermarket (all season). General shop. Kiosk. Restaurant and takeaway (1/7-31/8). Bar and snacks (all season). Swimming pools, bathing caps compulsory (20/5-15/9). Entertainment organised with a soundproofed pub/disco (July/Aug). Gym park. Tennis. Playground. Hairdresser (July/Aug). Torches necessary in some areas. Animals are not accepted. Off site: Bicycle hire and large sports complex with multiple facilities including an indoor pool 1 km. Sailing and boat launching 10 km. Riding and golf 20 km.

Open: 26 March - 26 September.

Directions: From A8 (Bilbao - Santander) take km. 185 exit and N634 towards Beranga. Almost immediately turn right on CA147 to Noja. In 10 km. turn left at multiple campsite signs and go through town. At beach follow signs to site. GPS: 43.48948, -3.53700

Charges guide

Per person	€ 4,20 - € 6,40
child (3-9 yrs)	€ 3,00 - € 4,80
pitch incl. electricity	€ 18,60 - € 32,00

No credit cards.

Orbitur São Pedro de Moel

Rua Volta do Sete, P-2430 São Pedro de Moel (Leiria)
t: 244 599 168   e: info@orbitur.pt
alanrogers.com/PO8100   www.orbitur.pt

Accommodation: ☑Pitch ☑Mobile home/chalet   ☐Hotel/B&B ☐Apartment

This quiet and very attractive site is situated under tall pines, on the edge of the rather select small resort of São Pedro de Moel. This is a shady site which can be crowded in July and August. The 525 pitches are in blocks and unmarked (cars may be parked separately) with 404 electrical connections. A few pitches are used for permanent units. Although there are areas of soft sand, there should be no problem in finding a firm place. The large restaurant and bar are modern as is the superb swimming pool, paddling pool and flume (there is a lifeguard). The attractive, sandy beach is a short walk downhill from the site (you can take the car, although parking may be difficult in the town) and is sheltered from the wind by low cliffs.

You might like to know
The sheltered beach is only 500 m. away from the campsite.

☐ Beach on site
☑ Beach within 1 km.

☑ Sandy beach

☐ Blue Flag quality

☐ Lifeguard *(high season)*

☐ Sun lounger/deckchair hire

☑ Watersports
(e.g. sailing, windsurfing)

☑ Snacks and drinks

☑ Sunshades

☐ Dogs allowed *(on the beach)*

Facilities: Four clean toilet blocks have mainly British style toilets (some with bidets), some washbasins with hot water. Hot showers are mostly in one unisex block. Motorcaravan services. Gas supplies. Laundry. Supermarket. Large restaurant and bar with terrace (closed in November). Swimming pools (1/3-30/9). Satellite TV. Games room. Playground. Tennis. WiFi. Off site: Bus service 100 m. Beach 500 m. Fishing 1 km.

Open: All year.

Directions: Site is 9 km. west of Marinha Grande, on the right as you enter São Pedro de Moel. GPS: 39.75883, -9.02229

Charges guide

Per person	€ 5,10
child (5-10 yrs)	€ 2,60
pitch	€ 10,90 - € 11,90
electricity	€ 2,90 - € 3,50

Off season discounts (up to 70%).

PORTUGAL – Lagos

Camping Turiscampo

N125, Espiche, Luz, P-8600 Lagos (Faro)
t: 282 789 265 e: info@turiscampo.com
alanrogers.com/PO8202 www.turiscampo.com

Accommodation: ☑Pitch ☑Mobile home/chalet ☐Hotel/B&B ☐Apartment

This good quality site has been thoughtfully refurbished and updated since it was purchased by the friendly Coll family, who are known to us from their previous Spanish site. The site provides 347 pitches for touring units, mainly in rows of terraces, all with electricity and some with shade. They vary in size (70-120 m²). The upper areas of the site are mainly used for bungalow accommodation (and are generally separate from the touring areas). A new, elevated Californian style pool plus a children's pool have been constructed. The supporting structure is a clever water cascade and surround and there is a large sun lounger area on astroturf. One side of the pool area is open to the road. The restaurant/bar has been tastefully refurbished and Roberto and his staff are delighted to use their excellent English, while providing good fare at most reasonable prices. The restaurant has two patios, one of which is used for live entertainment in season. The sea and the city of Lagos, with all the attractions of the Algarve, are within easy reach. This is a very good site for families and for 'Snowbirds' to over-winter.

You might like to know
The campsite is 4 km. from Lagos and a little further is Portimão, both of which offer superb sandy beaches.

☐ Beach on site
☑ Beach within 1 km.
☑ Sandy beach
☐ Blue Flag quality
☐ Lifeguard (high season)
☐ Sun lounger/deckchair hire
☑ Watersports
  (e.g. sailing, windsurfing)
☑ Snacks and drinks
☐ Sunshades
☐ Dogs allowed (on the beach)

Facilities: Four toilet blocks are well located around the site. Two have been refurbished, two are new and contain modern facilities for disabled campers. Hot water throughout. Facilities for children. Washing machines. Shop. Gas supplies. Restaurant/bar. Swimming pool (March-Oct) with two terraces. Bicycle hire. Entertainment in high season on the bar terrace. Playground on sand. Adult art workshops. Aqua gymnastics. Miniclub (5-12 yrs) in season. Boules. Archery. Sports field. Cable TV. Internet. WiFi on payment. Bungalows to rent. Off site: Bus to Lagos and other towns from Praia da Luz village 1.5 km. Fishing and beach 2 km. Golf 4 km. Sailing 5 km. Boat launching 5 km. Riding 10 km.

Open: All year.

Directions: Take exit 1 from the N125 Lagos - Vila do Bispo. The impressive entrance is about 3 km. on the right. GPS: 37.10111, -8.73278

Charges guide

Per person	€ 3,10 - € 6,20
child (3-10 yrs)	€ 1,70 - € 3,10
pitch	€ 5,90 - € 13,70
electricity (6/10A)	€ 3,00 - € 4,00
dog	€ 1,00 - € 1,50

PORTUGAL – Quarteira

Orbitur Camping Quarteira

Estrada da Fonte Santa, avenida Sá Cameiro, P-8125-618 Quarteira (Faro)
t: 289 302 826   e: info@orbitur.pt
alanrogers.com/PO8220   www.orbitur.pt

Accommodation: ☑Pitch ☑Mobile home/chalet   ☐Hotel/B&B   ☐Apartment

This is a large, busy, attractive site on undulating ground with some terracing, taking 795 units. On the outskirts of the popular Algarve resort of Quarteira, it is 600 m. from a sandy beach which stretches for a kilometre to the town centre. Many of the unmarked pitches have shade from tall trees and a few small individual pitches of 50 m². with electricity and water can be reserved. There are 659 electrical connections. Like others along this coast, the site encourages long winter stays. There is a large restaurant and supermarket which have a separate entrance for local trade. The swimming pools (free for campers) are excellent, featuring pools for adults (with a large flume) and children (with fountains).

You might like to know

The city of Faro is a bus ride away – the bus leaves from outside the campsite gate or alternatively visit Almancil to the São Lournco Church.

☐ Beach on site
☑ Beach within 1 km.
☑ Sandy beach
☐ Blue Flag quality
☐ Lifeguard *(high season)*
☑ Sun lounger/deckchair hire
☑ Watersports
  (e.g. sailing, windsurfing)
☑ Snacks and drinks
☑ Sunshades
☐ Dogs allowed *(on the beach)*

Facilities: Five toilet blocks provide British and Turkish style toilets, washbasins with cold water, hot showers plus facilities for disabled visitors. Washing machines. Motorcaravan services. Gas. Supermarket. Self-service restaurant (closed Nov). Takeaway (from late May). Swimming pools (Apr-Sept). General room with bar and satellite TV. WiFi. Tennis. Open-air disco (high season). Off site: Bus from gate to Faro. Fishing 1 km. Bicycle hire (summer) 1 km. Golf 4 km.

Open: All year.

Directions: Turn off N125 for village of Almancil. In the village take road south to Quarteira. Site is on the left 1 km. after large, official town welcome sign. GPS: 37.06666, -8.08333

Charges guide

Per person	€ 5,90
child (5-10 yrs)	€ 3,00
pitch	€ 12,70 - € 13,70
electricity	€ 2,90 - € 3,50

Off season discounts (up to 70%).

ITALY – Grado

Camping Tenuta Primero

Via Monfalcone 14, I-34073 Grado (Friuli - Venézia Giúlia)
t: 043 189 6900 e: info@tenuta-primero.com
alanrogers.com/IT60065 www.tenuta-primero.com

Accommodation: ☑Pitch ☑Mobile home/chalet ☐Hotel/B&B ☐Apartment

Tenuta Primero was established in 1962 and has been a popular family site ever since. The third generation of the Marzola family continue to run the site and have made many improvements over the years. This is a large site with its own private beach and 800 pitches of varying sizes, including some new, large 'executive' pitches, with beach front locations, 10A electricity and a private water supply. Nine toilet blocks are dispersed around the site, some equipped with facilities for disabled visitors. There are no fewer than three restaurants here (including a pizzeria and a fish restaurant) and two bars, as well as a separate disco. Alongside the campsite is a large private marina with moorings for over 200 boats and a maintenance area. Tenuta Primero also comprises an 18-hole championship golf course and a nine-hole executive course. Special rates are available for campers. Grado is a fascinating resort 5 km. away. The old town predates Venice and has a similar appeal.

You might like to know
If you feel like a change from the beach, why not take a day trip to Venice?

☑ **Beach on site**
☐ **Beach within 1 km.**

☑ **Sandy beach**
☑ **Blue Flag quality**
☑ **Lifeguard** *(high season)*
☑ **Sun lounger/deckchair hire**
☑ **Watersports**
  (e.g. sailing, windsurfing)
☑ **Snacks and drinks**
☑ **Sunshades**
☐ **Dogs allowed** *(on the beach)*

Facilities: Supermarket. Bars and restaurants. Pizzeria. Swimming and paddling pools. Disco. Beauty salon. Aerobics. Windsurfing and sailing lessons. Play area. Sports pitches. Bicycle hire. Entertainment and activity programme. Children's activities. Direct access to beach. Mobile homes and chalets for rent. Dogs are not accepted. Off site: Campsite harbour. Two golf courses. Cycle track to Grado. Shops, restaurants and bars in Grado. Riding 2 km.

Open: 1 April - 4 October.

Directions: Take the Palmanova exit from the A4 autostrada and drive to Grado on the SS352 passing through Aquileia and Cervignano. Continue towards Monfalcone on the SP19 and the site can be found on the right after 5 km. GPS: 45.7051, 13.4640

Charges guide

Per person	€ 5,00 - € 11,00
child (3-11 yrs)	free - € 7,00
child (12-15 yrs)	€ 4,00 - € 9,00
pitch incl. electricity	€ 10,00 - € 25,00

ITALY – Bibione

Villaggio Turistico Internazionale

Via Colonie 2, I-30020 Bibione (Veneto)
t: 043 144 2611 e: info@vti.it
alanrogers.com/IT60140 www.vti.it

Accommodation: ☑Pitch ☑Mobile home/chalet ☐Hotel/B&B ☑Apartment

This is a large, professionally run tourist village which offers all a holidaymaker could want. The Granzotto family have owned the site since the sixties and the results of their continuous improvements are impressive. There are 350 clean pitches, many fully serviced, shaded by mature trees and mostly on flat ground. The site's large sandy beach is excellent (umbrellas and loungers available for a small charge), as are all the facilities within the campsite where English speaking, uniformed assistants will help when you arrive. The tourist village is split by a main road with the main restaurant, cinema and children's club on the very smart chalet side. The professional hairdressing salon sets the luxurious tone of the site. A comprehensive entertainment programme is on offer daily and the large pool provides a great flume and slides and a separate fun and spa pool. The local area is a major tourist resort but for more relaxation try the famous thermal baths at Bibione!

You might like to know
On the beach you will find 340 sun umbrellas and sun beds together with 4 lifeguards. There is also a sailing and surfing school. Boats and surf boards can be hired.

- ☑ Beach on site
- ☐ Beach within 1 km.

- ☑ Sandy beach
- ☑ Blue Flag quality
- ☑ Lifeguard *(high season)*
- ☑ Sun lounger/deckchair hire
- ☑ Watersports
  (e.g. sailing, windsurfing)
- ☑ Snacks and drinks
- ☑ Sunshades
- ☐ Dogs allowed *(on the beach)*

Facilities: Four modern toilet blocks house excellent facilities with mainly British style toilets. Excellent provision for children and disabled campers. Air conditioning in all accommodation. Washing machines and dryers. Motorcaravan service point. Supermarket. Bazaar. Good restaurant with bright yellow plastic chairs. Snack bar. New pool complex. Fitness centre. Disco. TV. Cinema and theatre. Internet. Play areas. Tennis. Electronic games. Renovated apartments. Off site: Bicycle hire 1 km. Riding 3 km. Golf 6 km. Fishing.

Open: 1 April - 26 September.

Directions: Leave A4 east of Venice at Latisana exit on Latisana road. Then take road 354 towards Ligmano, after 12 km. turn right to Beuazzana and then left to Bibione. Site is well signed on entering town.
GPS: 45.6351, 13.0374

Charges guide

Per unit incl. 2 persons and electricity	€ 19,00 - € 42,00
extra person	€ 5,00 - € 10,50
child (1-5 yrs)	free - € 8,00
dog	€ 7,00

ITALY – Cavallino-Treporti

Camping Union Lido Vacanze

Via Fausta 258, I-30013 Cavallino-Treporti (Veneto)
t: 041 257 5111   e: info@unionlido.com
alanrogers.com/IT60200   www.unionlido.com

Accommodation: ☑Pitch ☑Mobile home/chalet ☐Hotel/B&B ☐Apartment

This amazing site is very large, offering everything a camper could wish for. It is extremely well organised and it has been said to set the standard that others follow. It lies right beside the sea with direct access to a long, broad sandy beach which shelves very gradually and provides very safe bathing (there are lifeguards). The site itself is regularly laid out with parallel access roads under a covering of poplars, pine and other trees providing good shade. There are 2,600 pitches for touring units, all with electricity and 1,684 also have water and drainage. You really would not need to leave this site – everything is here, including a sophisticated Wellness centre. There are two aqua parks, one with fine sand beaches (a first in Europe). A huge selection of sports is offered, along with luxury amenities too numerous to list. Entertainment and fitness programmes are organised in season. Union Lido is above all an orderly and clean site, which is achieved by reasonable regulations to ensure quiet, comfortable camping and by good management. Member of Leading Campings Group.

You might like to know

One of Europe's largest sites, looking straight out to the Adriatic with a long private beach (1,200 metres), Union Lido is a top quality holiday centre with a wide range of amenities.

- ☑ **Beach on site**
- ☐ Beach within 1 km.
- ☑ **Sandy beach**
- ☑ **Blue Flag quality**
- ☑ **Lifeguard** (high season)
- ☑ **Sun lounger/deckchair hire**
- ☑ **Watersports** (e.g. sailing, windsurfing)
- ☑ **Snacks and drinks**
- ☑ **Sunshades**
- ☐ **Dogs allowed** (on the beach)

Facilities: Fifteen well kept, fully equipped toilet blocks which open and close progressively during the season. Facilities for disabled people. Launderette. Motorcaravan service points. Gas supplies. Comprehensive shopping areas set around a pleasant piazza (all open till late). Eight restaurants each with a different style. Nine pleasant and lively bars. Impressive aquaparks (from 15/5). Tennis. Riding. Minigolf. Skating. Bicycle hire. Archery. Two fitness tracks. Golf academy. Diving centre and school. Windsurfing school in season. Boat excursions. Recreational events. Hairdressers. Internet cafés. ATM. Dogs are not accepted. Off site: Boat launching 3.5 km. Aqualandia (special rates).

Open: 30 April - 26 September (with all services).

Directions: From Venice - Trieste autostrada leave at exit for airport or Quarto d'Altino and follow signs first for Jésolo and then Punta Sabbioni, and site will be seen just after Cavallino on the left. GPS: 45.46788, 12.53036

Charges guide

Per unit incl. 2 persons and electricity	€ 25,40 - € 60,00
extra person	€ 6,60 - € 10,50
child (1-11 yrs)	€ 3,70 - € 8,80

Three different seasons.

Camping Vela Blu

Via Radaelli 10, I-30013 Cavallino-Treporti (Veneto)
t: 041 968 068   e: info@velablu.it
alanrogers.com/IT60280   www.velablu.it

Accommodation: ☑Pitch ☑Mobile home/chalet ☐ Hotel/B&B ☐ Apartment

Thoughtfully landscaped within a natural wooded coastal environment, the tall pines here give shade while attractive flowers enhance the setting and paved roads give easy access to the pitches. The 280 pitches vary in size (55-100 m²) and shape, but all have electricity (10A) and 80 have drainage. Vela Blu is a relatively new, small, family style site and a pleasant alternative to the other massive sites on Cavallino. The clean, fine sand beach runs the length of one side of the site with large stone breakwaters for fun and fishing. The beach is fenced, making it safer for children, with access via a gate and there are lifeguards in season. There are outdoor showers and footbaths. The hub of the site is the charming restaurant and brilliant play area on soft sand, both adjoining a barbecue terrace and entertainment area. A well stocked shop is also in this area. For those who enjoy a small quiet site, Vela Blu fits the bill. Venice is easy to access as is the local water park (there is no pool here as yet).

You might like to know

The fine sandy beach alongside the site is now reserved exclusively for the site guests where you will find sunshades, loungers, kiosks and beach volleyball.

☑ **Beach on site**
☐ **Beach within 1 km.**

☑ **Sandy beach**
☑ **Blue Flag quality**
☑ **Lifeguard** *(high season)*
☑ **Sun lounger/deckchair hire**
☑ **Watersports**
    (e.g. sailing, windsurfing)
☑ **Snacks and drinks**
☑ **Sunshades**
☐ **Dogs allowed** *(on the beach)*

Facilities: Two excellent modern toilet blocks include baby rooms and good facilities for disabled visitors. An attendant is on hand to maintain high standards. Laundry facilities. Motorcaravan service point. Medical room. Shop. Bar. Gelateria. Restaurant and takeaway. Games room. Satellite TV room. Pedalos. Windsurfing. Fishing. Bicycle hire. Entertainment. Off site: Bars, restaurants and shops. Ferry to Venice. Theme parks.

Open: 19 April - 25 September.

Directions: Leave A4 Venice - Trieste motorway at exit for 'Aeroporto' and follow signs for Jésolo and Punta Sabbioni. Site is signed after village of Cavallino. GPS: 45.45681, 12.5072

Charges guide

Per person	€ 4,00 - € 8,00
child (1-10 yrs)	free - € 8,00
seniors (over 60)	€ 3,10 - € 7,00
pitch incl. all services	€ 8,50 - € 17,00

Camping dei Fiori

Via Pisani 52, I-30013 Cavallino-Treporti (Veneto)
t: **041 966 448** e: **fiori@vacanze-natura.it**
alanrogers.com/IT60300 www.deifiori.it

Accommodation: ☑Pitch ☑Mobile home/chalet ☐ Hotel/B&B ☐ Apartment

Dei Fiori stands out amongst the other small sites in the area. As its name implies, it is ablaze with colourful flowers and shrubs in summer and presents a neat and tidy appearance whilst providing a quiet atmosphere. The 350 touring pitches, with electricity (6/10A), are either in woodland where space varies according to the trees which have been left in their natural state, or under artificial shade where regular shaped pitches are of reasonable size. Well built bungalows for rent enhance the site and are in no way intrusive, giving a village-like effect. About a quarter of the pitches are taken by static units, many for rent. Shops and a restaurant are in the centre next to the swimming pools. Nearby is the hydro-massage bath which is splendidly appointed and reputed to be the largest in Italy. The long beach is of fine sand and shelves gently into the sea. Regulations ensure the site is quiet between 23.00-07.30 and during the afternoon siesta period. Venice is about 40 minutes away by bus and boat, and excursions are arranged. The site is well maintained by friendly, English speaking management.

Special offers
Boats for rent. Diving school (PADI). Boat excursions (organised by PADI) to discover the underwater rock formations and the naval wrecks of the last wars.

You might like to know
Every year during the month of August, 'Beach on Fire', the largest show of fireworks in the world, takes place all along the seashore of Cavallino-Treporti.

☑ **Beach on site**
☐ **Beach within 1 km.**
☑ **Sandy beach**
☑ **Blue Flag quality**
☑ **Lifeguard** *(high season)*
☐ **Sun lounger/deckchair hire**
☑ **Watersports**
  (e.g. sailing, windsurfing)
☑ **Snacks and drinks**
☑ **Sunshades**
☐ **Dogs allowed** *(on the beach)*

Facilities: Three sanitary blocks are of exceptional quality with well equipped baby rooms, good facilities for disabled people and washing machines and dryers. Family rooms (key from reception). Motorcaravan services. Shops. Restaurant. Snack bar. Satellite TV. Swimming pools and whirlpool. Fitness centre, hydro-massage bath (charged in mid and high seasons) and activity programmes (1/5-30/9). Tennis. Minigolf. Play area. Organised activities, entertainment and excursions. Bicycle hire. Internet and WiFi. Dogs are not accepted. Off site: Public transport 200 m. Riding 4 km. Fishing 7 km. Golf 15 km.

Open: 22 April - 30 September.

Directions: Leave A4 Venice - Trieste autostrada either by taking exit for airport or Quarto d'Altino and follow signs for Jesolo and then Punta Sabbioni and site signs just after Ca'Ballarin. GPS: 45.45263, 12.47127

Charges guide

Per person	€ 4,70 - € 9,80
child (6-12 yrs) or senior (over 65 yrs)	€ 3,90 - € 8,60
pitch	€ 9,00 - € 24,00
tent pitch incl. electricity	€ 7,40 - € 19,00

Min. stay 3 days in high season (3/7-21/8).

Camping Ca'Pasquali

Via A Poerio 33, I-30013 Cavallino-Treporti (Veneto)
t: 041 966 110 e: info@capasquali.it
alanrogers.com/IT60360 www.capasquali.it

Accommodation: ☑Pitch ☑Mobile home/chalet ☐ Hotel/B&B ☐ Apartment

Situated on the attractive natural woodland coast of Cavallino with its wide, safe, sandy beach, Ca'Pasquali is a good quality holiday resort with easy access to magnificent Venice. This is an ideal place for a holiday interspersed with excursions to Verona, Padova, the glassmakers of Murano, the local water park, pretty villages and many other cultural attractions. This is a large site and detail is important here; there are superb pools, a fitness area, an arena for an ambitious entertainment programme and a beachside restaurant. The 400 pitches are shaded and flat (70-90 m²), and some have spectacular sea views. The fine sandy beach was alive with families playing games, flying kites and enjoying themselves when we watched from the thoughtfully renovated restaurant as the sun set. A family site with many extras, Ca'Pasquali has been thoughtfully designed to a high standard – it is ideal for families as a resort holiday or to combine with sightseeing.

You might like to know

The beach next to the site is now reserved exclusively for the site guests and has beach umbrellas, sun loungers, kiosks, beach volleyball and table tennis. A 40 minute boat ride will take you to Venice.

☑ Beach on site
☐ Beach within 1 km.

☑ Sandy beach
☑ Blue Flag quality
☑ Lifeguard *(high season)*
☑ Sun lounger/deckchair hire
☑ Watersports
  (e.g. sailing, windsurfing)
☑ Snacks and drinks
☑ Sunshades
☐ Dogs allowed *(on the beach)*

Facilities: Three spotless modern units have excellent facilities with superb amenities for disabled campers and babies. Washing machines and dryers. Motorcaravan services. Restaurant. Pizzeria. Crêperie. Cocktail bar. Snack bar. Supermarket. Bazaar. Boutique. Superb pool complex with slides, fun pool and fountains. Fitness centre. Play areas. Bicycle hire. Canoe hire and lessons. Excellent entertainment. Amphitheatre. Miniclub. Internet access. Excursion service. Caravan storage. Dogs and other animals are not accepted. Off site: Golf and riding 5 km. Sailing 20 km. Fishing. Theme parks.

Open: 14 April - 30 September.

Directions: Leave autostrada A4 at Noventa exit in San Doná di Piave and head towards Jesolo and to Cavallino - Treporti. Site is well signed shortly after town of Cavallino.
GPS: 45.45237, 12.48905

Charges guide

Per unit incl. 2 persons and electricity	€ 17,20 - € 43,50
extra person	€ 4,30 - € 9,50
child (1-10 yrs)	free - € 9,50

Camping Village Garden Paradiso

Via Baracca 55, I-30013 Cavallino-Treporti (Veneto)
t: 041 968 075   e: info@gardenparadiso.it
alanrogers.com/IT60400   www.gardenparadiso.it

Accommodation: ☑ Pitch ☑ Mobile home/chalet ☐ Hotel/B&B ☐ Apartment

There are many sites in this area and there is much competition in providing a range of facilities. Garden Paradiso is a good seaside site which also provides three excellent, centrally situated pools, a fitness centre, minigolf, a train to the market and other activities for children. Compared with other sites here, this one is of medium size with 776 pitches. All have electricity (4/6A), water and drainage points and all are marked and numbered with hard access roads, under a good cover of trees. Many flowers and shrubs give a pleasant and peaceful appearance and a new reception provides a professional welcome. The restaurant, with self-service at lunch time and waiter service at night, is near the beach with a bar/snack bar in the centre of the site. The site is directly on the sea with a beach of fine sand. A community bus service runs daily to the local markets. The site is used by tour operators (35 pitches).

You might like to know

The fine sandy beach slopes gently down to the sea and twice a week the pirate ship, Jolly Roger, sails from here. There are children's slides and swings, and beach volleyball.

☑ **Beach on site**
☐ **Beach within 1 km.**

☑ **Sandy beach**
☐ **Blue Flag quality**

☑ **Lifeguard** *(high season)*
☑ **Sun lounger/deckchair hire**
☑ **Watersports**
   (e.g. sailing, windsurfing)
☑ **Snacks and drinks**
☑ **Sunshades**
☐ **Dogs allowed** *(on the beach)*

Facilities: Four brick, tiled toilet blocks are fully equipped with a mix of British and Turkish style toilets. Facilities for babies. Washing machines and dryers. Motorcaravan services. Shopping complex. Restaurant (23/4-30/9). Snack bar and takeaway. 'Aqualandia' pool complex (charged). Fitness centre. Tennis. Minigolf. Play area. Organised entertainment and excursions (high season). Bicycle hire. WiFi. Dogs are not accepted. Off site: Riding 2 km. Fishing 2.5 km.

Open: 23 April - 30 September.

Directions: Leave Venice - Trieste autostrada either by taking airport or Quarto d'Altino exits; follow signs to Jesolo and Punta Sabbioni. Take first road left after Cavallino roundabout and the site is a little way on the right.
GPS: 45.47897, 12.56359

Charges guide

Per unit incl. 2 persons, electricity, water and drain	€ 20,10 - € 43,20
extra person	€ 4,80 - € 9,50
child (6-12 yrs) or senior (over 61 yrs)	€ 3,25 - € 7,30
child (3-5 yrs)	free - € 6,30

Less 10% for stays over 30 days (early), or 20 days (late) season.

ITALY – Cavallino-Treporti

Camping Village Europa

Via Fausta 332, I-30013 Cavallino-Treporti (Veneto)
t: 041 968 069 e: info@campingeuropa.com
alanrogers.com/IT60410 www.campingeuropa.com

Accommodation: ☑Pitch ☑Mobile home/chalet ☐Hotel/B&B ☐Apartment

Europa has a great position with direct access to a fine sandy beach with lifeguards. There are 411 touring pitches, all with 8A electricity, some with water, drainage and satellite TV connections. There is a separate area for campers with dogs and some smaller pitches are available for those with tents. The site is kept beautifully clean and neat and there is an impressive array of restaurants, bars, shops and leisure amenities. These are cleverly laid out along an avenue and include a jewellers, a doctor's surgery, Internet services and much more. Leisure facilities are arranged around the site. A professional team provides entertainment and regular themed 'summer parties'. Some restaurant tables have pleasant sea views. Venice is easily accessible by bus and then ferry from Punta Sabbioni.

You might like to know
The long, wide beach of very fine sand is cleaned on a daily basis, features natural dunes and is ideal for young children.

☑ Beach on site
☐ Beach within 1 km.

☑ Sandy beach
☑ Blue Flag quality
☑ Lifeguard *(high season)*
☑ Sun lounger/deckchair hire
☑ Watersports
   (e.g. sailing, windsurfing)
☑ Snacks and drinks
☑ Sunshades
☐ Dogs allowed *(on the beach)*

Facilities: Three superb toilet blocks are kept pristine and have hot water throughout. Facilities for disabled visitors. Washing machines. Large supermarket and shopping centre. Bars, cafés, restaurants and pizzeria. New 'aqua park' with slide and spa centre. Tennis. Games room. Playground. Children's clubs. Entertainment programme. Internet access. Direct access to the beach. Windsurf and pedalo hire. Mobile homes and chalets for rent. Off site: Riding and boat launching 1 km. Golf and fishing 2 km. ATM 500 m. Walking and cycling trails. Excursions to Venice.

Open: 4 April - 30 September.

Directions: From A4 autostrada (approaching from Milan) take Mestre exit and follow signs initially for Venice airport and then Jésolo. From Jesolo, follow signs to Cavallino from where site is well signed. GPS: 45.47380, 12.54903

Charges guide

Per person	€ 4,00 - € 7,90
child (2-5 yrs)	€ 3,00 - € 6,90
adult over 60 yrs	€ 3,40 - € 7,80
pitch	€ 8,20 - € 20,50
dog	€ 2,00 - € 4,50

No credit cards.

ITALY – Lévico Terme

Camping Lévico

Localitá Pleina 5, I-38056 Lévico Terme (Trentino - Alto Adige)
t: 046 170 6491   e: mail@campinglevico.com
alanrogers.com/IT62290   www.campinglevico.com

Accommodation: ☑Pitch ☑Mobile home/chalet ☐Hotel/B&B ☐Apartment

Sister site to Camping Jolly, Camping Lévico is in a natural setting on the small, very pretty Italian lake also called Lévico which is surrounded by towering mountains. The sites are owned by two brothers – Andrea, who manages Lévico, and Gino, based at Jolly. Both campsites are charming. Lévico has some pitches along the lake edge and a quiet atmosphere. There is a shaded terrace for enjoying pizza and drinks in the evening. Pitches are of a good size, most grassed and well shaded with 6A electricity. Staff are welcoming and fluent in many languages including English. There is a small supermarket on site and it is a short distance to the local village. The beautiful grass shores of the lake are ideal for sunbathing and the crystal clear water is ideal for enjoying (non-motorised) water activities. This is a site where the natural beauty of an Italian lake can be enjoyed without being overwhelmed by commercial tourism. All the amenities at Camping Jolly can be enjoyed by traversing a very pretty walkway along a stream where we saw many trout.

You might like to know

Large private beach. The clear, shallow waters of the lake offer opportunities for swimming, fishing, canoeing, and boating. You can rent canoes and pedal boats from reception.

☑ **Beach on site**

☐ **Beach within 1 km.**

☐ **Sandy beach**

☑ **Blue Flag quality**

☑ **Lifeguard** (high season)

☑ **Sun lounger/deckchair hire**

☑ **Watersports**
 (e.g. sailing, windsurfing)

☑ **Snacks and drinks**

☑ **Sunshades**

☐ **Dogs allowed** (on the beach)

Facilities: Four modern sanitary blocks provide hot water for showers, washbasins and washing. Mostly British style toilets. Single locked unit for disabled visitors. Washing machines and dryer. Ironing. Freezer. Motorcaravan service point. Bar/restaurant, takeaway and good shop. Play area. Miniclub and entertainment (high season). Fishing. Satellite TV and cartoon cinema. Internet access. Kayak hire. Tennis. Torches useful. Off site: Town 2 km. with all the usual facilities and ATM. Bicycle hire 1.5 km. and bicycle track. Boat launching 500 m. Riding 3 km. Golf 7 km.

Open: 1 April - 11 October.

Directions: From A22 Verona - Bolzano road take turn for Trento on S47 to Lévico Terme where campsite is very well signed. GPS: 46.00799, 11.28454

Charges guide

Per person	€ 5,00 - € 9,50
child (3-11 yrs)	€ 4,00 - € 6,00
pitch incl. electricity (6A)	€ 7,50 - € 18,00

ITALY – Framura

Camping Framura

Localitá La Spiaggetta, I-19014 Framura (Ligúria)
t: **018 781 5030** e: **hotelriviera@hotelrivieradeivamarina.it**
alanrogers.com/IT64180

Accommodation: ☑Pitch ☑Mobile home/chalet ☑Hotel/B&B ☐Apartment

Framura is an unusual, small cliff-side site of 160 pitches including just 12 pitches for touring units. These pitches are wedged in between seasonal units and are on the site of the old railway line, as is the whole steeply terraced site. The pitches themselves are fabulous as they are directly above the crystal clear waters here. Access to the site is through an old railway tunnel and there is absolutely no shade. The supporting amenities are basic but have a certain charm, some being cut into the rock face. The site is unsuitable for children, the infirm and has no facilities for disabled campers. It might suit the more adventurous camper who needs little support and enjoys a challenge. One permanent pitch is a charming 20 m. railway carriage. The site is twinned with the Hotel Riviera through the tunnel and the pleasant restaurant here can be used if you have missed the supermarket in town.

You might like to know
The sandy beach with clean, crystal clear sea is backed by rocky areas and lends itself to coastal walks. Also suitable for diving.

☑ **Beach on site**

☐ **Beach within 1 km.**

☑ **Sandy beach**

☐ **Blue Flag quality**

☐ **Lifeguard** (high season)

☐ **Sun lounger/deckchair hire**

☐ **Watersports**
    (e.g. sailing, windsurfing)

☑ **Snacks and drinks**

☐ **Sunshades**

☐ **Dogs allowed** (on the beach)

Facilities: Five very mixed blocks offer basic toilets, mostly Turkish but some British style. Innovation has been used here and one very small shower block is carved into the rock face. Cold water at sinks. Washing machine. Very basic snack bar and takeaway (1/6-15/9). Bar (1/4-30/10). Small shop (15/6-15/9). Canoeing and windsurfing are possible. Fishing. Dogs are not accepted. Off site: Boat launching 1 km. Bicycle hire 3 km.

Open: 1 April - 30 October.

Directions: From A12 take nearest exit to Deiva Marina (depending on approach direction) east of Portofino. Exciting stuff now! Proceed to the town centre. Take care to find the campsite signs as the road to the north is impassable for larger units! Cross the narrow bridge and test your skill down the narrow approach road with the Italian parking. You end up facing a narrow railway tunnel. Take a breath, check for cyclists in the dark interior and drive through to the site! GPS: 44.21670, 9.56440

Charges guide

Per person	€ 8,50 - € 10,50
child (4-12 yrs)	€ 6,00 - € 8,00
pitch	€ 6,00 - € 13,50
electricity	€ 1,00

Baia Domizia Villaggio Camping

I-81030 Baia Domizia (Campania)
t: 082 393 0164   e: info@baiadomizia.it
alanrogers.com/IT68200   www.baiadomizia.it

Accommodation: ☑Pitch ☑Mobile home/chalet ☐Hotel/B&B ☐Apartment

This large, beautifully maintained seaside site is about 70 kilometres northwest of Naples, and is within a pine wood, cleverly left in its natural state. Although it does not feel like it, there are 750 touring pitches in clearings, either of grass and sand or on hardstanding, all with electricity. Most pitches are well shaded, however there are some in the sun for cooler periods. The central complex is superb with well designed buildings providing for all needs (the site is some distance from the town). Restaurants, bars and a 'gelaterie' enjoy live entertainment and attractive water lily ponds surround the area. Near the entrance is a new swimming pool complex complete with hydromassage points and a large sunbathing area. The supervised beach is of soft sand and a great attraction. Although the site is big, there is never very far to walk to the beach, and although it may be some 300 m. to the central shops and restaurant from the site boundaries, there is always a nearby toilet block. Member of Leading Campings Group.

You might like to know
There is a large solarium on the beach. A variety of day excursions include trips to Rome and the Isle of Capri.

- ☑ **Beach on site**
- ☐ **Beach within 1 km.**
- ☑ **Sandy beach**
- ☐ **Blue Flag quality**
- ☐ **Lifeguard** (high season)
- ☑ **Sun lounger/deckchair hire**
- ☐ **Watersports** (e.g. sailing, windsurfing)
- ☐ **Snacks and drinks**
- ☑ **Sunshades**
- ☐ **Dogs allowed** (on the beach)

Facilities: Seven new toilet blocks have hot water in washbasins (many cabins) and showers. Good access and facilities for disabled people. Washing machines, spin dryers. Motorcaravan services. Gas supplies. Supermarket and general shop. Large bar. Restaurants, pizzeria and takeaway. Ice cream parlour. Swimming pool complex. Playground. Tennis. Bicycle hire. Windsurfing hire and school. Disco. Excursions. Torches required in some areas. Dogs are not accepted. Off site: Fishing and riding 3 km.

Open: 30 April - 20 September.

Directions: The turn to Baia Domizia leads off the Formia - Naples road 23 km. from Formia. From Rome - Naples autostrada, take Cassino exit to Formia. Site is to the north of Baia Domizia and well signed. Site is off the coastal road that runs parallel to the SS7.
GPS: 41.207222, 13.791389

Charges guide

Per person	€ 5,10 - € 11,20
child (1-11 yrs)	€ 4,00 - € 8,50
pitch incl. electricity	€ 11,50 - € 23,00

ITALY – Aglientu

Camping Baia Blu La Tortuga

Pineta di Vignola Mare, I-07020 Aglientu (Sardinia)
t: 079 602 200   e: info@baiablu.com
alanrogers.com/IT69550   www.baiaholiday.com

Accommodation: ☑Pitch ☑Mobile home/chalet ☐Hotel/B&B ☐Apartment

In the northeast of Sardinia and well situated for the Corsica ferry, Baia Blu is a large, professionally run campsite. The beach with its golden sand, brilliant blue sea and pretty rocky outcrops is warm and inviting. The site's 304 touring pitches, and almost as many mobile homes (most with air conditioning), are of fine sand and shaded by tall pines with banks of colourful oleanders and wide boulevards providing good access for units. Four exceptionally good toilet blocks provide a good ratio of excellent facilities to pitches including some combined private shower/washbasin cabins for rent. This is a busy, bustling site with lots to do and attractive restaurants. There is a new bar/restaurant area with gazebos, a more casual beachside restaurant and bar, plus a self-service restaurant. The site is very popular with Italian families who enjoy the wide range of amenities here. It is used by many tour operators.

You might like to know
To the left of the bay is a beach of white sand. At the other end, there are rocks and opportunities for those who love fishing.

☑ Beach on site
☐ Beach within 1 km.

☑ Sandy beach
☐ Blue Flag quality
☐ Lifeguard *(high season)*
☑ Sun lounger/deckchair hire
☐ Watersports
  (e.g. sailing, windsurfing)
☐ Snacks and drinks
☑ Sunshades
☐ Dogs allowed *(on the beach)*

Facilities: Four excellent blocks (two with solar panels for hot water) with free hot showers, WCs, bidets and washbasins. Facilities for disabled people. Washing machines and dryers. Motorcaravan services. Supermarket. Gas. Bazaar. New bar and restaurant. Beachside restaurant and bar. Self-service restaurant. Snack bar and takeaway. Gym. Hairdresser. Doctor's surgery. Playground. Tennis. Games and TV rooms. Windsurfing and diving schools. Internet point and WiFi area. Massage centre. Entertainment and sports activities (mid May-Sept). Excursions. Barbecue area (not permitted on pitches). Off site: Disco 50 m. Riding 18 km.

Open: 1 April - 18 October.

Directions: Site is on the north coast between towns of Costa Paradiso and S. Teresa di Gallura (18 km) at Pineta di Vignola Mare and is well signed. GPS: 41.12611, 9.06722

Charges guide

Per unit incl. 2 persons, water and electricity	€ 17,00 - € 49,00
tent pitch incl. electricity	€ 14,00 - € 39,00
extra person	€ 2,00 - € 12,00
child (3-9 yrs)	€ 2,00 - € 9,50
dog	€ 3,50 - € 8,00

Camping Areti

GR-63081 Neos Marmaras (Central Macedonia)
t: **237 507 1430** e: **info@camping-areti.gr**
alanrogers.com/GR8145 www.camping-areti.gr

Accommodation: ☑Pitch ☑Mobile home/chalet ☐ Hotel/B&B ☐ Apartment

If you imagine a typical Greek campsite as being set immediately behind a small sandy beach in a quiet cove with pitches amongst pine and olive trees which stretch a long way back to the small coast road, then you have found your ideal site. Camping Areti is beautifully located just off the beaten track on the peninsula of Sithonia. It has 130 pitches for touring units. The olive groves at the rear provide hidden parking spaces for caravans and boats. Small boats can be launched from the beach. The Charalambidi family maintain their site to very high standards and this is a site where visitors will not be disappointed. Olive, pine and eucalyptus trees provide shade for the grass pitches and when we visited in June, there was a wonderful display of cacti in full bloom near the entrance. This site, with its quiet, picturesque location, good facilities and friendly management has won many well-deserved recommendations and represents camping at its best. It is the ideal place to spend some time after the long journey to Greece.

You might like to know

The 'Spalathronisia', three small islands ideal for excursions and fishing, are located at a distance of only 300 m. from the beach.

☐ **Beach on site**

☑ **Beach within 1 km.**

☑ **Sandy beach**

☐ **Blue Flag quality**

☐ **Lifeguard** (high season)

☐ **Sun lounger/deckchair hire**

☑ **Watersports**
  (e.g. sailing, windsurfing)

☑ **Snacks and drinks**

☐ **Sunshades**

☐ **Dogs allowed** (on the beach)

Facilities: Three excellent toilet blocks include showers, WCs and washbasins. Kitchen with sinks, electric hobs and fridges. Laundry with washing machines. Chemical disposal. Small shop and restaurant. Sandy beach. Bungalows to rent. Fishing, sailing and swimming. Communal barbecue area. Off site: Riding, golf and bicycle hire 10 km. Sithonia, Mount Athos and the nearby Spalathronissia islands.

Open: 1 May - 31 October.

Directions: Although the postal address is Neos Marmaras the site is 12 km. south. So stay on the main coast road, past the casino resort at Porto Carras and 5 km. further on turn right towards the site (signed). Then turn right again down to the coast and turn left and on for 1.5 km. Turn right into site access road. Reception is 700 m. GPS: 40.024183, 23.81595

Charges guide

Per unit incl. 2 persons and electricity	€ 33,70 - € 37,00

No credit cards.

GREECE – Nafplio

Camping New Triton

Plaka Drepano, GR-21060 Nafplio (Peloponnese)
t: 275 209 2128
alanrogers.com/GR8635

Accommodation: ☑ Pitch ☐ Mobile home/chalet ☐ Hotel/B&B ☐ Apartment

What do we look for in a good campsite in Greece? Given the excellent Greek weather, the answer is probably a good, flat pitch with some shade, excellent toilets and showers that are spotlessly clean, a small shop and proximity to a beach and local tavernas. Well, here you have it all! Under the control of the owners, Mr. and Mrs. George Christopoulous, this is an exceptional site with 40 good size touring pitches under high screens, just across the road from Drepano beach. Local tavernas are within strolling distance and the town's shops are about a mile away. Personal management and supervision clearly works and this small site sets very high standards that others often fail to achieve.

You might like to know
Close to the Drepano beach there are small pool areas where blue and white cranes live and breed. Deprano village is 1.2 km. away where you will find tavernas and local bars.

☐ Beach on site
☑ Beach within 1 km.
☑ Sandy beach
☐ Blue Flag quality
☐ Lifeguard *(high season)*
☐ Sun lounger/deckchair hire
☑ Watersports
  (e.g. sailing, windsurfing)
☐ Snacks and drinks
☑ Sunshades
☐ Dogs allowed *(on the beach)*

Facilities: Excellent refurbished toilet blocks include showers, WCs and washbasins. Baby bath. Facilities for disabled visitors. Chemical disposal. Laundry with washing machines and ironing board. Electric hobs for cooking. Fridge and freezer. Small shop (1/6-30/9). Off site: Drepano beach, local tavernas and bars. Assini.

Open: 1 April - 30 October.

Directions: From Nafplio follow the main road west and then turn right towards Drepano. In the town follow the signs Plaka Drepano and turn left towards the coast. At the beach turn right and site is just ahead. GPS: 37,53202, 22.80165

Charges guide

Per unit incl. 2 persons and electricity   € 23,00

46

GREECE – Finikounda

Camping Finikes

GR-24006 Finikounda (Peloponnese)
t: 272 302 8524 e: camping-finikes@otenet.gr
alanrogers.com/GR8695 www.finikescamping.gr

Accommodation: ☑Pitch ☑Mobile home/chalet ☐Hotel/B&B ☐Apartment

This site offers 80 level pitches with good shade and great views. It also has
16 apartments to rent. Some pitches have high reed screens that give good protection
from the blazing Greek sun and the turquoise sea is great for swimming, windsurfing
and sailing. The site is at the western corner of Finikounda Bay and has direct access
to the sandy beach by crossing small natural dunes. The facilities are excellent and
in low season, when there are 18 or less campers, each camper is given the keys
to a WC and shower for their own personal use. The small picturesque village,
two kilometres to the east, is at the back of the bay. Caiques and fishing boats are
drawn up all along the sandy shore here, while tavernas serve the freshly caught fish.

You might like to know

There is an attractive path across the dunes
from the site to the beach which is excellent
for children. The town of Finikounda is
a 20 minute walk along the beach.

☑ **Beach on site**

☐ **Beach within 1 km.**

☑ **Sandy beach**

☐ **Blue Flag quality**

☐ **Lifeguard** *(high season)*

☐ **Sun lounger/deckchair hire**

☑ **Watersports**
   (e.g. sailing, windsurfing)

☐ **Snacks and drinks**

☐ **Sunshades**

☐ **Dogs allowed** *(on the beach)*

Facilities: The good toilet block includes
showers, WCs and washbasins. Facilities for
disabled visitors. Kitchen includes sinks, electric
hobs and fridges. Laundry. Chemical disposal.
Bar, small shop and restaurant. Accommodation
to rent. Off site: Finikounda and the Inouse
Islands.

Open: All year.

Directions: Site is 2 km. from the centre of
Finikounda. From the village head west and turn
left into the site. GPS: 36.802817, 21.78105

Charges guide

Per person	€ 5,50 - € 6,00
child (4-12 yrs)	€ 3,00 - € 3,50
pitch incl. car	€ 6,50 - € 8,50
electricity	€ 3,50

No credit cards.

GREECE – Pylos

Camping Navarino Beach

Gialova, GR-24001 Pylos (Peloponnese)
t: 272 302 2973 e: info@navarino-beach.gr
alanrogers.com/GR8705 www.navarino-beach.gr

Accommodation: ☑Pitch ☑Mobile home/chalet ☐ Hotel/B&B ☐ Apartment

There are 150 pitches, most facing the beach, with 30 being directly situated alongside. All have electricity (10A) and most have good shade. The pitches are arranged in rows to ensure that all have beach access. The facilities are adequate and cleaned regularly. The staff are friendly and efficient, and there is a very good restaurant with a terrace directly by the beach. The light wind in the morning which strengthens on some afternoons makes it a great windsurfing location and boats can be moored directly by the beach. This site is highly recommended. Situated directly on the beach in the historic Bay of Navarino, there can be very few sites that have the wonderful position this one occupies; it is superb and has the most amazing sunset to complement that. The site, which has plenty of shade, is split into two with the second section across the road used mainly for tents or as overspill. The beach is sandy and shelves gently making it incredibly safe for children.

Facilities: The five toilet blocks are well situated and, even in high season, were kept very clean and never became overcrowded. Small shop where basic provisions can be purchased. Other shops within walking distance. Dogs are accepted but must be kept on a lead and out of the sea. Off site: Within walking distance of Gialova with its promenade restaurants. Pylos 6 km, Nestors Palace 12 km. Numerous places to visit.

Open: All year, full facilities Easter - October.

Directions: Directly on the National Road Pylos Kyparissia. 300 m. from the village of Gialova. GPS: 36.94764, 21.70618

Charges guide

Per unit incl. 2 persons and electricity	€ 23,00 - € 25,00
extra person	€ 6,00
child	€ 3,00

You might like to know
The blue shallow water on this sandy beach is safe for children. The campsite recommend a visit to the Divary Lagoon which is considered to be one of the most important lagoons in Greece.

- ☑ **Beach on site**
- ☐ **Beach within 1 km.**
- ☑ **Sandy beach**
- ☐ **Blue Flag quality**
- ☐ **Lifeguard** *(high season)*
- ☐ **Sun lounger/deckchair hire**
- ☑ **Watersports**
    (e.g. sailing, windsurfing)
- ☐ **Snacks and drinks**
- ☑ **Sunshades**
- ☐ **Dogs allowed** *(on the beach)*

CROATIA – Porec

Camping Lanterna

Lanterna, HR-52440 Porec (Istria)
t: 052 465 010 e: camping@valamar.com
alanrogers.com/CR6716 www.camping-adriatic.com

Accommodation: ☑Pitch ☑Mobile home/chalet ☐Hotel/B&B ☐Apartment

This is one of the largest sites in Croatia with an amazing selection of activities and high standards and is part of the 'Camping on the Adriatic' group. Reception is buzzing in high season as around 10,000 guests are on site. Set in 90 hectares with over 3 km. of beach, there are 3,000 pitches of which 2,600 are for touring units. The pitches are 60-120 m² in size with some superb locations right on the sea, although these tend to be taken first so it is advisable to book ahead. Some of the better pitches are in a 'reserved booking' area. Terracing has improved the view in many areas. Some of the marked and numbered pitches are shaded and arranged to take advantage of the topography. Electrical connections are 10A. Facilities at Lanterna are impressive with the whole operation running smoothly for the campers. The land is sloping in parts and terraced in others. There is a large pool and pretty bay with rocky beaches and buoyed safety areas. Many activities and quality entertainment for all are available both on and off site – you are spoilt for choice here, including a vast choice of places to eat.

You might like to know
There are more than 3 km. of beaches in the area.

☑ Beach on site
☐ Beach within 1 km.

☐ Sandy beach
☑ Blue Flag quality
☑ Lifeguard *(high season)*
☑ Sun lounger/deckchair hire
☑ Watersports
  (e.g. sailing, windsurfing)
☑ Snacks and drinks
☑ Sunshades
☑ Dogs allowed *(on the beach)*

Facilities: The fourteen sanitary blocks are clean and good quality. Children's facilities and baby care areas, some Turkish style WCs, hot showers, with some blocks providing facilities for disabled visitors. Three supermarkets sell most everyday requirements. Fresh fish shop. Four restaurants, bars and snack bars and fast food outlets. Swimming pool and two paddling pools. Sandpit and play areas, with entertainment for all in high season. Tennis. Bicycle hire. Watersports. Boat hire. Minigolf. Riding. Internet café. Jetty and ramp for boats. Dogs are restricted to a certain area. Off site: nearest large supermarket in Novigrad 9 km. Hourly bus service from the reception area. Fishing. Riding 500 m.

Open: 1 April - 15 October.

Directions: The turn to Lanterna is well signed off the Novigrad to Porec road about 8 km. south of Novigrad. Continue for about 2 km. down the turn off road towards the coast and the campsite is difficult to miss on the right hand side.
GPS: 45.29672, 13.59442

Charges guide

Per person	€ 3,85 - € 6,60
child (4-10 yrs)	free - € 4,65
pitch incl. electricity	€ 6,60 - € 12,25
incl. water	€ 8,35 - € 14,95

CROATIA – Porec

Naturist Resort Solaris

Lanterna bb, HR-52440 Porec (Istria)
t: 052 465 110   e: camping-porec@valamar.com
alanrogers.com/CR6718   www.camping-adriatic.com

Accommodation: ☑Pitch ☑Mobile home/chalet ☐Hotel/B&B ☐Apartment

This naturist site is part of the 'Camping on the Adriatic' group and has a most pleasant feel and when we visited in high season there were lots of happy people having fun. A pretty cove and lots of beach frontage with cool pitches under trees makes the site very attractive. Of the 1,445 pitches, 550 are available for touring, with 600 long stay units. There are 145 fully serviced pitches (100 m²) available on a first-come, first-served basis, with an ample supply of electricity hook-ups (10-16A) and plentiful water points. As this is a naturist site, single men and groups consisting of men only are prohibited and there are restrictions on photography. Ball games are forbidden in the camping areas. There is a small, but very pleasant swimming pool close to the restaurant which has a lifeguard (clothing is not allowed in the pool). For those who embrace the naturist regime or want to give it a try, this is a pleasant, quiet site with above average facilities in an area of outstanding natural beauty.

Facilities: Thirteen excellent, fully equipped toilet blocks provide toilets, washbasins and showers. Some blocks have facilities for disabled visitors. Washing machines and ironing facilities. Restaurants, grills and fast food. Supermarkets. Swimming pool. Tennis. Bicycle hire. Riding. Play areas. Boat launching. Car wash. Entertainment. Dogs are restricted to a particular area and are not allowed on the beach. Off site: Excursions. Riding and fishing 500 m.

Open: 1 April - 10 October.

Directions: Site is 3 km. off the Novigrad - Porec road about 8 km. south of Novigrad and is well signed. Camping Lanterna is also down this road so signs for this site may be followed also. GPS: 45.29126, 13.5848

Charges guide

Per person	€ 3,00 - € 6,15
child (4-10 yrs)	free - € 4,35
pitch incl. electricity	€ 6,10 - € 17,50
dog	€ 3,45 - € 4,90

Prices for pitches by the sea are higher.

You might like to know
Please note - this is a naturist campsite. Pets are only allowed in certain areas. Access to the sea is possible for disabled visitors.

☑ **Beach on site**
☐ Beach within 1 km.

☐ Sandy beach
☑ **Blue Flag quality**
☑ **Lifeguard** *(high season)*
☐ Sun lounger/deckchair hire
☑ **Watersports**
   (e.g. sailing, windsurfing)
☑ **Snacks and drinks**
☐ Sunshades
☑ **Dogs allowed** *(on the beach)*

CROATIA – Rovinj

Camping Polari

Polari bb, HR-52210 Rovinj (Istria)
t: 052 801 501   e: polari@maistra.hr
alanrogers.com/CR6732   www.CampingRovinjVrsar.com

Accommodation: ☑Pitch ☑Mobile home/chalet ☐Hotel/B&B ☐Apartment

This 60 hectare site has excellent facilities for both textile and naturist campers, the latter having a reserved area of 12 hectares called Punta Eva. Prime places are taken by permanent customers but there are some numbered pitches which are very good. Many of the pitches have been thoughtfully upgraded and now a new pitch (100 m²) is offered with full facilities. Pitches are clean, neat and level and there will be shade when the young trees grow. There is something for everyone here to enjoy or you may prefer just to relax. Enjoy a meal on the huge restaurant terrace with panoramic views of the sea. An impressive swimming pool complex is child friendly with large paddling areas. Part of the Maistia Group, the site has undergone a massive improvement programme and the result makes it a very attractive option.

You might like to know
Located on a picturesque cove with over two kilometres of attractive coastline and plentiful shade offering respite from the summer heat. New swimming pool and extensive sports provision.

☑ **Beach on site**
☐ **Beach within 1 km.**

☐ **Sandy beach**
☑ **Blue Flag quality**
☑ **Lifeguard** *(high season)*
☑ **Sun lounger/deckchair hire**
☑ **Watersports**
  (e.g. sailing, windsurfing)
☑ **Snacks and drinks**
☑ **Sunshades**
☑ **Dogs allowed** *(on the beach)*

Facilities: All the sanitary facilities have been renovated to a high standard with plenty of hot water and good showers. Washing machines and dryers. Laundry service including ironing. Motorcaravan service point. Two shops, one large and one small, one restaurant and snack bar. Tennis. Minigolf. Children's entertainment with all major European languages spoken. Bicycle hire. Watersports. Sailing school. Off site: Riding 1 km. Five buses daily to and from Rovinj 3 km. Golf 30 km.

Open: 1 April - 2 October.

Directions: From any access road to Rovinj look for red signs to AC Polari (amongst other destinations). The site is about 3 km. south of Rovinj. GPS: 45.06286, 13.67489

Charges guide

Per unit incl. 2 persons and electricity	€ 18,00 - € 40,80
extra person (18-64 yrs)	€ 5,00 - € 8,90
children and seniors according to age	free - € 8,50

For stays less than 3 nights in high season add 20%.

CROATIA – Fazana

Camping Bi-Village

Dragonja 115, HR-52212 Fazana (Istria)
t: 052 300 300   e: info@bivillage.com
alanrogers.com/CR6745   www.bivillage.com

Accommodation: ☑Pitch ☑Mobile home/chalet   ☐Hotel/B&B ☐Apartment

Camping Bi-Village is a large holiday village, close to the historic town of Pula and opposite the Brioni National Park. The location is excellent and there are some superb sunsets. The site is landscaped with many flowers, shrubs and rock walls and offers over 1,000 pitches for touring units (the remainder taken by bungalows and chalets). The campsite is separated from the holiday bungalows by the main site road which runs from the entrance to the beach. Pitches are set in long rows accessed by gravel lanes, slightly sloping towards the sea, with only the bottom rows having shade from mature trees and good views over the Adriatic. The pitches are separated by young trees and shrubs. Bi-Village has 800 m. of pebble beach, but also offers three attractive swimming pools with a fun pool, slides and flumes. In front of the touring pitches is a commercial centre with a supermarket and several restaurants and bars.

You might like to know
The campsite offers an extensive activities programme targeted at different age groups between 3 and 18 years. This includes courses in kayaking, windsurfing, football and even dance.

☑ Beach on site
☐ Beach within 1 km.

☐ Sandy beach
☑ Blue Flag quality

☐ Lifeguard *(high season)*

☑ Sun lounger/deckchair hire

☐ Watersports
   (e.g. sailing, windsurfing)

☐ Snacks and drinks

☑ Sunshades

☑ Dogs allowed *(on the beach)*

Facilities: Four modern toilet blocks with toilets, open plan washbasins and controllable hot showers. Child-size washbasins. Baby room. Facilities for disabled visitors. Washing machine. Shopping centre (1/5-11/10). Bars (1/5-30/9) and restaurants. Bazaar. Gelateria. Pastry shop. Three swimming pools. Playground on gravel. Playing field. Trampolines. Minigolf. Jet skis, motorboats and pedaloes for hire. Boat launching. Games hall. Sports tournaments and entertainment organised. Massage. Internet point. Off site: Historic towns of Pula and Rovinj are close. Fishing 3 km. Riding 15 km.

Open: 5 March - 31 October.

Directions: Follow no. 2 road south from Rijeka to Pula. In Pula follow site signs. Site is close to Fazana. GPS: 44.91717, 13.81105

Charges guide

Per person	€ 4,00 - € 8,50
child	free - € 4,50
pitch incl. electricity and water	€ 5,50 - € 16,00
dog	€ 2,00 - € 3,00

CROATIA – Primosten

Camp Adriatic

Huljerat bb, HR-22202 Primosten (Dalmatia)
t: 022 571 223 e: info@camp-adriatic.hr
alanrogers.com/CR6845 www.camp-adriatic.hr

Accommodation: ☑Pitch ☑Mobile home/chalet ☐Hotel/B&B ☐Apartment

As we drove south down the Dalmatian coast road, we looked across a clear turquoise bay and saw a few tents, caravans and motorcaravans camped under some trees.
A short distance later we were at the entrance of Camp Adriatic. With 530 pitches that slope down to the sea, the site is deceptive and enjoys a one kilometre beach frontage which is ideal for snorkelling and diving. Most pitches are level and have shade from pine trees. There are 212 numbered pitches and 288 unnumbered, all with 10/16A electricity. Close to the delightful town of Primosten (with a taxi boat service in high season) the site boasts good, modern amenities and a fantastic location.

You might like to know
The site boasts its own dive centre and can also organise boat trips and inland excursions to the beautiful Krka River National Park and the Skardinski Buk waterfalls.

☑ **Beach on site**

☐ **Beach within 1 km.**

☐ **Sandy beach**

☐ **Blue Flag quality**

☐ **Lifeguard** (high season)

☑ **Sun lounger/deckchair hire**

☑ **Watersports**
　(e.g. sailing, windsurfing)

☐ **Snacks and drinks**

☑ **Sunshades**

☐ **Dogs allowed** (on the beach)

Facilities: Four modern sanitary blocks provide clean toilets, hot showers and washbasins. Facilities for disabled visitors. Bathroom for children. Washing machine and dryer. Kitchen facilities. Small supermarket (15/5-30/9). Restaurant, bar and takeaway (all season). Sports centre. Miniclub. Beach. Diving school. Sailing school and boat hire. Entertainment in July/Aug. Internet point. Off site: Primosten 2.5 km. Sibenic 25 km. Riding 15 km.

Open: 1 May - 15 October.

Directions: Take the A1 motorway south and leave at the Sibenik exit. Follow the 33 road into Sibenik and then go south along the coast road (no. 8), signed Primosten. Site is 2.5 km. north of Primosten. GPS: 43.606517, 15.92095

Charges guide

Per person	Kn 34,00 - 60,00
child (3-12 yrs)	Kn 25,00 - 45,00
pitch incl. electricity	Kn 54,00 - 105,00
dog	Kn 18,00 - 32,00

Balatontourist Camping Napfény

Halász u. 5, H-8253 Révfülöp (Veszprem County)
t: 87 563 031   e: napfeny@balatontourist.hu
alanrogers.com/HU5370   www.balatontourist.hu

Accommodation: ☑Pitch ☑Mobile home/chalet ☐Hotel/B&B ☐Apartment

Camping Napfény, an exceptionally good site, is designed for families with children of all ages looking for an active holiday, and has a 200 m. frontage on Lake Balaton. The site's 395 pitches vary in size (60-110 m²) and almost all have shade – very welcome during the hot Hungarian summers – and 6/10A electricity. As with most of the sites on Lake Balaton, a train line runs just outside the site boundary. There are steps to get into the lake and canoes, boats and pedaloes for hire. An extensive entertainment programme is designed for all ages and there are several bars and restaurants of various styles. There are souvenir shops and a supermarket. In fact, you need not leave the site at all during your holiday, although there are several excursions on offer, perhaps to Budapest or to one of the many Hungarian spas, a trip over Lake Balaton or a traditional wine tour.

You might like to know
There are beaches at the lakeside where there are pedaloes and boats for hire. Fishing is also popular on the lake.

- ☑ **Beach on site**
- ☐ **Beach within 1 km.**
- ☐ **Sandy beach**
- ☐ **Blue Flag quality**
- ☐ **Lifeguard** *(high season)*
- ☐ **Sun lounger/deckchair hire**
- ☑ **Watersports**
  (e.g. sailing, windsurfing)
- ☐ **Snacks and drinks**
- ☐ **Sunshades**
- ☐ **Dogs allowed** *(on the beach)*

Facilities: The three excellent sanitary blocks have toilets, washbasins (open style and in cabins) with hot and cold water, spacious showers (both preset and controllable), child size toilets and basins, and two bathrooms (hourly charge). Heated baby room. Facilities for disabled people. Launderette. Dog shower. Motorcaravan services. Supermarket. Several bars, restaurants and souvenir shops. Sports field. Tennis. Minigolf. Fishing. Bicycle hire. Canoe, rowing boats and pedalo hire. Extensive entertainment programme for all ages. Free internet access. Off site: Riding 3 km.

Open: 30 April - 30 September.

Directions: Follow road 71 from Veszprém southeast to Keszthely. Site is in Révfülöp. GPS: 46.82417, 17.63733

Charges guide

Per unit incl. 2 persons and electricity	HUF 3400 - 7150
extra person	HUF 800 - 1200
child (2-14 yrs)	HUF 550 - 900
dog	HUF 550 - 900

Camping Campofelice

Via alle Brere 7, CH-6598 Tenero (Ticino)
t: **091 745 1417** e: **camping@campofelice.ch**
alanrogers.com/CH9890 **www.campofelice.ch**

Accommodation: ☑Pitch ☑Mobile home/chalet ☐Hotel/B&B ☐Apartment

The largest site in Switzerland, it is bordered on the front by Lake Maggiore and on one side by the Verzasca estuary, where the site has its own harbour. Campofelice is divided into rows, with 860 individual pitches of average size on flat grass on either side of hard access roads. Mostly well shaded, all pitches have electricity connections (10-13A) and some also have water, drainage and TV connections. Pitches near the lake cost more (these are not available for motorcaravans) and a special area is reserved for small tents. English is spoken at this good, if rather expensive, site. Sporting facilities are good and there are cycle paths in the area, including into Locarno. The beach by the lake is sandy, long and wider than the usual lakeside ones. It shelves gently so that bathing is safe for children. Water skiing and windsurfing facilities are 1 km. away.

You might like to know

The site is set on the sandy shores of Lake Maggiore where there is safe swimming and a private beach. Kayaks and canoes are available to hire from the sites own harbour.

☑ **Beach on site**

☐ **Beach within 1 km.**

☑ **Sandy beach**

☐ **Blue Flag quality**

☐ **Lifeguard** *(high season)*

☐ **Sun lounger/deckchair hire**

☐ **Watersports**
   (e.g. sailing, windsurfing)

☑ **Snacks and drinks**

☐ **Sunshades**

☐ **Dogs allowed** *(on the beach)*

Facilities: The six toilet blocks (one heated) are of excellent quality. Washing machines and dryers. Motorcaravan services. Gas supplies. Supermarket, restaurant, bar and takeaway (all season). Tennis. Minigolf. Bicycle hire. Playground. Doctor calls. Dogs are not accepted Off site: Fishing 500 m. Water skiing and windsurfing 1 km. Riding 5 km. Golf 8 km.

Open: 18 March - 31 October.

Directions: On the Bellinzona - Locarno road 13, exit Tenero. Site is signed at roundabout. GPS: 46.168611, 8.855556

Charges guide

Per unit incl. 2 persons

and electricity	€ 38,00 - € 82,00
extra person	€ 8,00 - € 11,00

Some pitches have minimum stay regulations.

FRANCE – Merville-Franceville

Camping les Peupliers

Allée des Pins, F-14810 Merville-Franceville (Calvados)
t: 02 31 24 05 07 e: asl-mondeville@wanadoo.fr
alanrogers.com/FR14190 www.camping-peupliers.com

Accommodation: ☑Pitch ☑Mobile home/chalet ☐Hotel/B&B ☐Apartment

Les Peupliers is run by friendly, family managers who keep this site attractive and tidy. It is just 300 metres from a long, wide, sandy beach. The touring pitches, of which there are 85, are on level open ground, all with 10A electricity. Those in the newest part are hedged but, with just a few trees on the edge of the site, there is little shade. The site amenities are near the entrance, housed in neat modern buildings. An animation programme for children and various activities are organised in high season. This site is ideally located for visiting Caen, Bayeux and the traditional seaside towns of Deauville and Trouville. The beaches in this area are plentiful and clean – a paradise for children. If sightseeing is on your agenda, many of the World War Two beaches and all the historical interest associated with D Day are within easy reach. At Deauville and Trouville, just a short distance away, you can soak up the atmosphere, perhaps spot a celebrity or two or relax on their beautiful beaches. You may, of course, prefer to stay on site and enjoy the facilities provided by the delightful managers.

You might like to know
There is a kite surfing school two kilometres away from the site. Sailing and kayaking activities are available three kilometres away.

☐ Beach on site

☑ Beach within 1 km.

☑ Sandy beach

☐ Blue Flag quality

☑ Lifeguard *(high season)*

☐ Sun lounger/deckchair hire

☐ Watersports
  (e.g. sailing, windsurfing)

☑ Snacks and drinks

☑ Sunshades

☑ Dogs allowed *(on the beach)*

Facilities: Two excellent heated toilet blocks with washbasins in cabins and showers. Good facilities for disabled visitors and for babies. Laundry room. Small shop, bar with terrace and takeaway (all July/Aug). Heated outdoor swimming pool and paddling pool (May-Sept). Play area. Games room. Entertainment in high season. WiFi. Off site: Fishing, riding and golf all within 1 km. Bicycle hire 2 km. Public transport 400 m.

Open: 1 April - 31 October.

Directions: From Ouistreham take the D514 to Merville-Franceville. Site is well signed off Allée des Pins. From Rouen on A13 (exit 29B), take D400 to Cabourg then the D514 to Merville-Franceville. GPS: 49.28326, -0.17053

Charges guide

Per unit incl. 2 persons and electricity	€ 20,10 - € 26,80
extra person	€ 5,55 - € 6,90

Camping Bois Soleil

2 avenue de Suzac, F-17110 Saint Georges-de-Didonne (Charente-Maritime)
t: 05 46 05 05 94   e: camping.bois.soleil@wanadoo.fr
alanrogers.com/FR17010   www.bois-soleil.com

Accommodation: ☑Pitch ☑Mobile home/chalet ☐Hotel/B&B ☐Apartment

Close to the sea, Bois Soleil is a large site in three parts, with 165 serviced pitches for touring units and a few for tents. All the touring pitches are hedged and have electricity, with water and drainage between two. The main part, Les Pins, is attractive with trees and shrubs providing shade. Opposite is La Mer with direct access to the beach, some areas with less shade and an area for tents. The third part, La Forêt, is for caravan holiday homes. Excellent private sanitary facilities are available to rent, either on your pitch or at a block (subject to availability). There are a few pitches with lockable gates. The areas are all well tended and are cleared and raked between visitors. This lively site offers something for everyone, whether it be a beach-side spot or a traditional pitch, plenty of activities or the quiet life. Recent additions include a new toilet block and some accommodation to rent with sea views. The wide sandy beach is popular with children and provides a pleasant walk to the pretty town of Saint Georges-de-Didonne.

You might like to know
Soak up all the flavours of the locality: seafood, oysters from Marennes-Oléron, Cognac's vineyards and the well-known Pineau des Charentes.

☑ **Beach on site**
☐ **Beach within 1 km.**

☑ **Sandy beach**
☐ **Blue Flag quality**
☐ **Lifeguard** (high season)
☐ **Sun lounger/deckchair hire**
☑ **Watersports**
  (e.g. sailing, windsurfing)
☑ **Snacks and drinks**
☐ **Sunshades**
☐ **Dogs allowed** (on the beach)

Facilities: Each area has one large and one small sanitary block. Heated block near reception. Cleaned twice daily, they include facilities for disabled people and babies. Launderette. Supermarket, bakery, beach shop (all 4/4-15/9). Restaurant, bar and takeaway (all 4/4-15/9). Swimming pool (heated 15/6-15/9). Steam room. Tennis. Bicycle hire. Play area. TV room and library. Internet terminal and WiFi. Charcoal barbecues not permitted. Dogs are not accepted 23/6-25/8. Off site: Fishing, riding 500 m. Golf 20 km.

Open: 4 April - 2 November.

Directions: From Royan centre take coast road (D25) along the seafront of St Georges-de-Didonne towards Meschers. Site is signed at roundabout at end of the main beach. GPS: 45.583583, -0.986533

Charges guide

Per unit incl. 2 persons, 6A electricity	€ 24,00 - € 39,00
tent incl. 2 persons	€ 18,00 - € 35,00
extra person	€ 3,00 - € 8,00
child (3-7 yrs)	free - € 6,00
dog (not 23/6-25/8)	€ 3,50

FRANCE – Saint Georges-d'Oléron

Camping les Gros Joncs

850 route de Ponthezieres, B.P. 17, F-17190 Saint Georges-d'Oléron (Charente-Maritime)
t: **05 46 76 52 29** e: **info@les-gros-joncs.fr**
alanrogers.com/FR17070 www.les-gros-joncs.fr

Accommodation: ☑Pitch ☑Mobile home/chalet ☐Hotel/B&B ☐Apartment

Situated on the west coast of the island of Ile d'Oléron, Les Gros Joncs is owned and run by the Cavel family who work hard to keep the site up-to-date and of high quality. There are 50 or so touring pitches of a good size (some extra large) with tall pine trees providing a choice between full sun and varying degrees of shade. All have water and 10A electricity to hand. The main building not only houses a light and airy reception, but also a modern, beautifully presented bar and restaurant, a fully stocked and well priced shop, a luxurious indoor swimming pool and a magnificent spa. The indoor pool, with water jets and jacuzzi, has glass sides which in good weather are opened out onto an outdoor pool area where there are also water slides, a paddling area and plenty of sunbathing terraces. Both pools are heated. The luxurious spa offers hydrotherapy and beauty treatments, sauna, and a comprehensive fitness room. Much attention has been given to the needs of disabled visitors here, including chalets where space and equipment are specially adapted. All amenities are of a standard unusual on a campsite.

You might like to know
The heated open-air pools include a toboggan, a large swimming pool and an adventure paddling pool. The indoor pool also has a whirlpool, lazy river, anatomical seats and powerful water jets.

☑ **Beach on site**
☑ **Beach within 1 km.**

☑ **Sandy beach**
☐ **Blue Flag quality**
☐ **Lifeguard** (high season)
☐ **Sun lounger/deckchair hire**
☐ **Watersports**
   (e.g. sailing, windsurfing)
☐ **Snacks and drinks**
☐ **Sunshades**
☐ **Dogs allowed** (on the beach)

Facilities: Traditional style toilet facilities are kept to a high standard. Laundry facilities. Motorcaravan services. Well stocked shop with bakery (1/4-15/9). Bar, restaurant and takeaway (all year). Indoor pool with first class spa and wellness centre (all year, with professional staff). Outdoor pool (heated, 1/4-15/9). Bicycle hire. Children's clubs (1/7-15/9). Internet access and WiFi. ATM. Barbecues are not permitted. Off site: Beach 200 m. or 400 m. via a sandy path. Bus service from Chéray. Fishing 2 km. Riding 6 km. Golf 8 km.

Open: All year.

Directions: Cross the viaduct onto the Ile d'Oléron. Take D734 (St Georges-d'Oléron). At traffic lights in Chéray turn left. Follow signs for camping and Sable Vignier. Soon signs indicate directions to Les Gros Joncs.
GPS: 45.95356, -1.37979

Charges guide

Per unit incl. 2 persons and electricity	€ 18,50 - € 45,50
extra person	€ 6,00 - € 11,80
child (0-7 yrs)	€ 2,70 - € 7,30
dog	€ 3,00

FRANCE – Royan-Pontaillac

Camping Clairefontaine

6 rue du Colonel Lachaud, F-17200 Royan-Pontaillac (Charente-Maritime)
t: 05 46 39 08 11 e: info@camping-clairefontaine.com
alanrogers.com/FR17100 www.camping-clairefontaine.com

Accommodation: ☑Pitch ☐ Mobile home/chalet ☐ Hotel/B&B ☐ Apartment

Camping Clairefontaine is situated on the outskirts of Royan, 300 m. from a golden sandy beach and casino. Although it is a busy area, the site is peaceful and relaxing. There are 300 pitches, of which 282 are available for touring. Electricity is available to all pitches, but some may require long leads. The site is mostly shaded and level with easy access to pitches. American motorhomes are accepted but care is needed on the entrance road to the site as it is not wide enough for two vehicles to pass. The reception area is large and welcoming and English is spoken. A programme of entertainment is provided in July and August and includes karaoke, singers and folk groups. There are many places of interest to visit, notably the nature reserves, the lighthouse at Cordouan, forests and the oyster beds of Marennes and Oléron.

You might like to know
Royan is the starting point for many great excursions – the Romanesque gems of the Saintonge, the Cognac countryside, the 17th-century Phare de Cordouan, the oysters of Marennes and the Gironde estuary.

☐ Beach on site
☑ Beach within 1 km.

☑ Sandy beach
☐ Blue Flag quality
☑ Lifeguard *(high season)*
☐ Sun lounger/deckchair hire
☑ Watersports
   (e.g. sailing, windsurfing)
☑ Snacks and drinks
☐ Sunshades
☐ Dogs allowed *(on the beach)*

Facilities: Two modern sanitary blocks. Good facilities for disabled visitors. Washing machines. Ironing room. Motorcaravan services. Shop. Bar. Restaurant with takeaway. Swimming and paddling pools. Four play areas. Tennis. Basketball. Entertainment in high season. Internet access. Off site: Beach and sailing 300 m. Bicycle hire 350 m. Fishing 2 km. Riding and golf 10 km.

Open: 24 May - 12 September.

Directions: Exit Royan on Avenue de Pontaillac towards La Palmyre. Turn right at the casino on the front, up Avenue Louise. Site is on left after 200 m. and is signed.
GPS: 45.631388, -1.050122

Charges guide

Per unit incl. 2 persons and electricity	€ 32,00 - € 35,00
extra person	€ 9,00 - € 9,50
child (2-10 yrs)	€ 5,00 - € 5,50
dog	€ 3,00

FRANCE – La Flotte-en-Ré

Camping les Peupliers

RD735, F-17630 La Flotte-en-Ré (Charente-Maritime)
t: 05 46 09 62 35 e: camping@les-peupliers.com
alanrogers.com/FR17290 www.camp-atlantique.com

Accommodation: ☑Pitch ☑Mobile home/chalet ☐ Hotel/B&B ☐ Apartment

On the Ile de Ré, you are never far from the sea and the location of this campsite is no exception. It is just 800 metres from the sea with sea views from some of the pitches. English is spoken at reception and the staff go out of their way to make your stay enjoyable. The 20 level touring pitches are in a separate area from 143 chalets for rent, in an area of light woodland. There are few water points. The trees provide some shade, but the very low hedges provide little privacy as the width and length of the pitches varies. The pitches are long enough for large units, including American motorhomes and twin axle caravans, although access to some pitches is difficult (prior booking necessary). The site is within walking distance of the shops and restaurants of the pretty fishing port of Flotte-en-Ré. With 100 km. of cycle tracks, sandy beaches, local markets and a uniquely sunny micro-climate, this a great place to sample island life. Historic La Rochelle on the mainland is one of France's most captivating ports.

You might like to know
The fine sandy beach is 800 m. from the site and is protected by the dunes and pine trees. Nearby in Flotte-en-Ré there is a sailing school, catamaran sailing trips and sea fishing.

☐ Beach on site

☑ Beach within 1 km.

☑ Sandy beach

☐ Blue Flag quality

☑ Lifeguard *(high season)*

☐ Sun lounger/deckchair hire

☑ Watersports
  (e.g. sailing, windsurfing)

☐ Snacks and drinks

☐ Sunshades

☐ Dogs allowed *(on the beach)*

Facilities: Two new but traditionally designed sanitary blocks are clean and well maintained. Both have unisex facilities including showers and vanity type units in cabins. Separate facilities for people with disabilities. Laundry facilities. Shop, restaurant, takeaway and bar with TV. Heated outdoor swimming pool (15/5-18/9). Play area. Children's club and entertainment (high season). Fridge hire. Bicycle hire. Max. 1 dog.
Off site: Riding 500 m. Beach, boat launching and sailing 800 m. Fishing 800 m. Golf 20 km.

Open: 3 April - 18 September.

Directions: Over the toll bridge and turn left at second roundabout. Site is well signed,
GPS: 46.182816, -1.30083

Charges guide

Per unit incl. 2 persons and electricity	€ 21,00 - € 33,00
extra person	€ 5,00 - € 8,00
child (0-5 yrs)	free - € 5,00
dog	€ 5,00

FRANCE – La Brée-les-Bains

Camping Antioche d'Oléron

Route de Proires, F-17840 La Brée-les-Bains (Charente-Maritime)
t: 05 46 47 92 00 e: info@camping-antiochedoleron.com
alanrogers.com/FR17570 www.camping-antiochedoleron.com

Accommodation: ☑Pitch ☑Mobile home/chalet ☐ Hotel/B&B ☐ Apartment

Situated to the northeast of the island, Camping Antioche is quietly located within a five minute walk to the beach. There are 130 pitches, of which 73 are occupied by mobile homes and 57 are for touring units. The pitches are set amongst attractive shrubs and palm trees and all have electricity (10A), water and a drain. A new pool area which comprises two swimming pools (heated), two jacuzzis, two paddling pools and a raised sunbathing deck, is beautifully landscaped with palms and flowers. A small bar, restaurant and takeaway offer reasonably priced food and drinks. The site becomes livelier in season with regular evening entertainment and activities for all the family. With specially prepared trails for cycling, oyster farms and salt flats to visit, the Ile d'Oléron offers something for everyone. Bresnais market, selling local produce and products, is within easy access on foot and is held daily in high season.

You might like to know
There is an area of the beach dedicated to watersports and pleasure boats. At low tide there is a flat rocky area ideal for fishing.

☐ Beach on site
☑ Beach within 1 km.

☑ Sandy beach

☐ Blue Flag quality

☑ Lifeguard *(high season)*

☐ Sun lounger/deckchair hire

☑ Watersports
   (e.g. sailing, windsurfing)

☑ Snacks and drinks

☐ Sunshades

☐ Dogs allowed *(on the beach)*

Facilities: The single sanitary block is of a good standard and is kept clean and fresh. Facilities for disabled visitors. Laundry. Motorcaravan services. Bar, restaurant and snack bar (weekends only May and June, daily July/Aug). Swimming and paddling pools. Games room. Play area. WiFi. Bicycle hire (July/Aug). Off site: Beach 150 m. Fishing 150 m. Riding 1.5 km. Golf 7 km.

Open: 1 April - 30 September.

Directions: Cross the bridge on the D26 and join the D734. After St Georges turn right onto the D273E1 towards La Brée-les-Baines. At T-junction turn left from where the campsite is signed. GPS: 46.02007, -1.35764

Charges guide

Per unit incl. 2 persons and electricity	€ 21,15 - € 35,15
extra person	€ 7,10
child (1-14 yrs)	€ 3,70
dog	€ 4,00

Camping Signol

121 avenue des Albatros, F-17190 Boyardville (Charente-Maritime)
t: 05 46 47 01 22   e: contact@signol.com
alanrogers.com/FR17600   www.signol.com

Accommodation: ☑Pitch ☑Mobile home/chalet ☐ Hotel/B&B ☐ Apartment

Occupying an eight-hectare site, just 800 metres from the sandy beaches, this campsite has plenty to offer. The 300 pitches are set amongst high pine trees and one metre high hedges give plenty of shade and privacy; some have sea views. The pitches are generous in size (80–120 m²) although access to some is tight and may not be suitable for larger units. Levelling blocks are required on some. Electricity (6A) is available to all, although long leads are required on a few pitches. Facilities for children are in a fenced area and include climbing frames, a bouncy castle and a multisport court. Heated swimming pools (supervised in high season) are overlooked by a bar and snack bar. A club for children is organised (July/August) and treasure hunts and other activities are organised daily. Entertainment for adults is also arranged in high season.

You might like to know

The beautiful fine sandy beaches of Boyardville are only 800 m. away, from where you have a wonderful view of Fort Boyard. Cycle tracks crisscross the oyster canals and Saumonards Forest.

☐ Beach on site

☑ Beach within 1 km.

☑ Sandy beach

☐ Blue Flag quality

☑ Lifeguard *(high season)*

☐ Sun lounger/deckchair hire

☐ Watersports
  (e.g. sailing, windsurfing)

☑ Snacks and drinks

☐ Sunshades

☐ Dogs allowed *(on the beach)*

Facilities: Three modern, fully equipped toilet blocks provide washbasins and showers in cubicles. They also include facilities for campers with disabilities and children. Laundry. Motorcaravan services. No shop. Bar/snack bar, terrace, takeaway, breakfast service. Two swimming pools, Enclosed play area with seats for parents. Children's club (from 1/7). Boules. Evening entertainment (from 1/7). WiFi (free). Dogs are not accepted in July/Aug. Barbecues are not allowed (communal area provided). Mobile homes and chalets available to hire. Off site: Nearest beach 800 m. Sailing and windsurfing. Fishing. Riding.

Open: 1 May - 12 September.

Directions: Cross the viaduct and continue on the D26 to Dolus and turn right on D126 signed Boyardville. Continue on this road for 6 km. until the canal bridge at the edge of the town. Cross bridge and turn immediately sharp right along the quayside. Site signed from here.
GPS: 45.96807, -1.24456

Charges guide

Per unit incl. 2 persons and electricity	€ 22,00 - € 34,60
extra person	€ 5,00 - € 8,50
child (under 7 yrs)	€ 4,00 - € 6,00

Camping du Letty

F-29950 Bénodet (Finistère)
t: 02 98 57 04 69   e: reception@campingduletty.com
alanrogers.com/FR29030   www.campingduletty.com

Accommodation: ☑Pitch ☑Mobile home/chalet ☐ Hotel/B&B ☐ Apartment

The Guyader family have ensured that this excellent and attractive site has plenty to offer for all the family. With a charming ambience, the site on the outskirts of the popular resort of Bénodet spreads over 22 acres with 493 pitches, all for touring units. Groups of four to eight pitches are set in cul-de-sacs with mature hedging and trees to divide each group. Most pitches have electricity, water and drainage. Although there is no swimming pool here, the site has direct access to a small sandy beach, and has provided a floating pontoon (safe bathing depends on the tides). At the attractive floral entrance, former farm buildings provide a host of facilities including an extensively equipped fitness room and new 'wellness' rooms for massage and jacuzzis. There is also a modern, purpose built nightclub and bar providing high quality live entertainment most evenings (situated well away from most pitches to avoid disturbance).

You might like to know

Letty is beside 'la Mer Blanche' which empties and fills with the rhythm of the tides – a haven for birds. Paradise for walkers and nature lovers. Wonderful sandy beaches.

☑ **Beach on site**
☐ **Beach within 1 km.**

☑ **Sandy beach**

☐ **Blue Flag quality**

☐ **Lifeguard** *(high season)*

☐ **Sun lounger/deckchair hire**

☑ **Watersports**
   (e.g. sailing, windsurfing)

☑ **Snacks and drinks**

☐ **Sunshades**

☑ **Dogs allowed** *(on the beach)*

Facilities: Six well placed toilet blocks are of good quality and include mixed style WCs, washbasins in large cabins and controllable hot showers (charged). Baby rooms. Separate facility for disabled visitors. Launderette. Hairdressing room. Motorcaravan service points. Well stocked shop. Extensive snack bar and takeaway. Bar with games room and night club. Library/reading room with four computer stations. Entertainment room with satellite TV. Fitness centre (no charge). Saunas, jacuzzi and solarium (all charged). Tennis and squash (charged). Boules. Archery. Well equipped play area. Entertainment and activities (July/Aug). WiFi in reception. Off site: Sailing, fishing, riding and golf all nearby.

Open: 15 June - 6 September.

Directions: From N165 take D70 Concarneau exit. At first roundabout take D44 to Fouesnant. Turn right at T-junction. After 2 km. turn left to Fouesnant (still D44). Continue through La Forêt Fouesnant and Fouesnant, picking up signs for Bénodet. Shortly before Bénodet at roundabout turn left (signed Le Letty). Turn right and site is 500 m. on left. GPS: 47.86700, -4.08783

Charges guide

Per person	€ 4,00 - € 6,50
child (1-6 yrs)	€ 2,00 - € 3,25
pitch incl. electricity	€ 12,50 - € 15,00

Camping le Panoramic

Route de la Plage-Penker, F-29560 Telgruc-sur-Mer (Finistère)
t: **02 98 27 78 41** e: **info@camping-panoramic.com**
alanrogers.com/FR29080 www.camping-panoramic.com

Accommodation: ☑Pitch ☑Mobile home/chalet ☐ Hotel/B&B ☐ Apartment

This medium sized, traditional site is situated on quite a steep, ten-acre hillside with fine views. It is personally run by M. Jacq and his family who all speak good English. The 200 pitches are arranged on flat, shady terraces, in small groups with hedges and flowering shrubs, and 20 pitches have services for motorcaravans. Divided into two parts, the main upper site is where most of the facilities are located, with the swimming pool, its terrace and a playground located with the lower pitches across the road. Some up-and-down walking is therefore necessary, but this is a small price to pay for such pleasant and comfortable surroundings. This area provides lovely coastal footpaths. The sandy beach and a sailing school at Trez-Bellec-Plage are a 700 m. walk. A Sites et Paysages member.

Special offers
01/05-14/07, 21/08-15/09: 2 people with car, caravan, 6A electricity = € 15/night.

You might like to know
A stay at the Panoramic means calm, relaxation and large pitches with panoramic views to the beach and the Bay of Douarnenez.

☐ Beach on site

☑ Beach within 1 km.

☑ Sandy beach

☐ Blue Flag quality

☐ Lifeguard *(high season)*

☐ Sun lounger/deckchair hire

☑ Watersports
(e.g. sailing, windsurfing)

☑ Snacks and drinks

☐ Sunshades

☐ Dogs allowed *(on the beach)*

Facilities: The main site has two well kept toilet blocks with another very good block opened for main season across the road. All three include British and Turkish style WCs, washbasins in cubicles, facilities for disabled people, baby baths, plus laundry facilities. Motorcaravan services. Small shop (1/7-31/8). Refurbished bar/restaurant with takeaway (1/7-31/8). Barbecue area. Heated pool, paddling pool and jacuzzi (1/6-15/9). Playground. Games and TV rooms. Tennis. Bicycle hire. WiFi. Off site: Beach and fishing 700 m. Riding 6 km. Golf 14 km. Sailing school nearby.

Open: 1 May - 15 September.

Directions: Site is just south of Telgruc-sur-Mer. On D887 pass through Sainte Marie du Ménez Horn. Turn left on D208 signed Telgruc-sur-Mer. Continue straight on through town and site is on right within 1 km. GPS: 48.22409, -4.37186

Charges guide

Per unit incl. 2 persons and electricity	€ 25,10 - € 26,50
extra person	€ 5,00
child (under 7 yrs)	€ 3,00
dog	€ 2,00

FRANCE – Névez

Camping le Raguenès-Plage

19 rue des Iles, F-29920 Névez (Finistère)
t: **02 98 06 80 69** e: **info@camping-le-raguenes-plage.com**
alanrogers.com/FR29090 **www.camping-le-raguenes-plage.com**

Accommodation: ☑Pitch ☑Mobile home/chalet ☐ Hotel/B&B ☐ Apartment

Mme. Guyader and her family will ensure you receive a warm welcome on arrival at this well kept and pleasant site. Le Raguenès-Plage is an attractive and well laid out campsite with many shrubs and trees. The 287 pitches are a good size, flat and grassy, separated by trees and hedges. All have electricity, water and drainage. The site is used by two tour operators (81 pitches), and has 49 mobile homes of its own. A pool complex complete with a new heated indoor pool and water toboggan is a key feature and is close to the friendly bar, restaurant, shop and takeaway. From the far end of the campsite a delightful five minute walk along a path and through a cornfield takes you down to a pleasant, sandy beach looking out towards the Ile Verte and the Presqu'île de Raguenès.

You might like to know
New heated, covered pool now open. Separate outdoor pool, also heated and with water slide and paddling pool.

☑ **Beach on site**
☐ **Beach within 1 km.**

☑ **Sandy beach**
☑ **Blue Flag quality**
☐ **Lifeguard** *(high season)*
☐ **Sun lounger/deckchair hire**
☑ **Watersports**
    (e.g. sailing, windsurfing)
☑ **Snacks and drinks**
☐ **Sunshades**
☐ **Dogs allowed** *(on the beach)*

Facilities: Two clean, well maintained sanitary blocks include mixed style toilets, washbasins in cabins, baby baths and facilities for disabled visitors. Laundry room. Motorcaravan service point. Small shop (from 15/5). Bar and restaurant (from 1/6) with outside terrace and takeaway. Reading and TV room, internet access point. Heated indoor and outdoor pools with sun terrace and paddling pool. Sauna (charged). Play areas. Games room. Various activities are organised in July/Aug. WiFi (charged). Off site: Beach, fishing and watersports 300 m. Supermarket 3 km. Riding 4 km.

Open: 1 April - 30 September.

Directions: From N165 take D24 Kerampaou exit. After 3 km. turn right towards Nizon and bear right at church in village following signs to Névez (D77). Continue through Névez, following signs to Raguenès. Continue for 3 km. to site entrance on left (entrance is quite small and easy to miss). GPS: 47.79337, -3.80049

Charges guide

Per unit incl. 2 persons and electricity	€ 20,00 - € 36,80
extra person	€ 4,40 - € 5,90
child (under 7 yrs)	€ 2,20 - € 3,70
dog	€ 1,50 - € 3,20

FRANCE – Le Guilvinec

Yelloh! Village la Plage

F-29730 Le Guilvinec (Finistère)
t: 02 98 58 61 90 e: info@yellohvillage-la-plage.com
alanrogers.com/FR29110 www.villagelaplage.com

Accommodation: ☑Pitch ☑Mobile home/chalet ☐Hotel/B&B ☐Apartment

La Plage is a spacious site located beside a long sandy beach between the fishing town of Le Guilvinec and the watersports beaches of Penmarc'h on the southwest tip of Brittany. It is surrounded by tall trees which provide shelter and is made up of several flat, sandy meadows. The 410 pitches (100 for touring units) are arranged on either side of sandy access roads, mostly not separated but all numbered. There is less shade in the newer areas. Electricity is available on most pitches. Like all beach-side sites, the facilities receive heavy use. There is plenty to occupy one at this friendly site but the bustling fishing harbour at Le Guilvinec and the watersports of Penmarc'h and Pointe de la Torche are within easy travelling distance.

Special offers
Specially adapted mobile homes for disabled visitors. Free children's club in high season. Free WiFi.

You might like to know
The wide variety of activities here includes 'initiation à la crêpe' and cycle trips along the coast. Also – thalassotherapy and archery.

☑ Beach on site
☐ Beach within 1 km.

☑ Sandy beach
☐ Blue Flag quality
☑ Lifeguard *(high season)*
☐ Sun lounger/deckchair hire
☑ Watersports
   (e.g. sailing, windsurfing)
☑ Snacks and drinks
☑ Sunshades
☑ Dogs allowed *(on the beach)*

Facilities: Four sanitary blocks are of differing designs but all provide modern, bright facilities including washbasins in cabins, good facilities for children and disabled people. Laundry facilities. Motorcaravan service point. Shop with gas supplies. Bright, airy, well furnished bar, crêperie and takeaway (all open all season). Covered heated swimming pool with paddling pool and slide. Sauna and fitness complex. Play area. TV room. Tennis. Minigolf. Petanque. Giant chess/draughts. Bicycle hire. Beach. Multisport and football fields. Entertainment all season. Off site: Fishing and watersports nearby. Riding 5 km. Golf 20 km.

Open: 2 April - 12 September.

Directions: Site is west of Guilvinec. From Pont l'Abbé, take the D785 road towards Penmarc'h. In Plomeur, turn left on D57 signed Guilvinec. On entering Guilvinec fork right signed Port and camping. Follow road along coast to site on left. GPS: 47.8025, -4.3072

Charges guide

Per unit incl. 2 persons and 6A electricity	€ 15,00 - € 40,00
extra person	€ 5,00 - € 7,00
child (under 10 yrs)	free - € 5,00
electricity (10A)	€ 1,00

FRANCE – Landéda

Camping des Abers

Dunes de Sainte Marguerite, F-29870 Landéda (Finistère)
t: 02 98 04 93 35 e: camping-des-abers@wanadoo.fr
alanrogers.com/FR29130 www.camping-des-abers.com

Accommodation: ☑Pitch ☑Mobile home/chalet ☐Hotel/B&B ☐Apartment

This delightful 12 acre site is in a beautiful location almost at the tip of the Presqu'île Sainte Marguerite on the northwestern shores of Brittany. The peninsula lies between the mouths (abers) of two rivers, Aber Wrac'h and Aber Benoît. Camping des Abers is set just back from a wonderful sandy beach with rocky outcrops and islands you can walk to at low tide. There are 180 pitches, landscaped and terraced, some with amazing views, others sheltered by mature hedges, trees and flowering shrubs. Hubert le Cuff makes you very welcome and speaks excellent English. This extensive site was created out of nothing by the le Cuff family who have tended it with loving care over the years. It is arranged on different levels avoiding any regimentation or crowding. Easily accessed by good internal roads, electricity is available to all. With its soft, white sandy beach the setting is ideal for those with younger children and this quiet, rural area provides a wonderful, tranquil escape from the hustle and bustle of life, even in high season.

You might like to know
There is a sailing club five minutes drive from the site and on the nearby estuary there are oyster farms and a bird sanctuary.

☑ Beach on site
☐ Beach within 1 km.

☑ Sandy beach
☐ Blue Flag quality
☐ Lifeguard (high season)
☐ Sun lounger/deckchair hire
☑ Watersports
   (e.g. sailing, windsurfing)
☐ Snacks and drinks
☐ Sunshades
☐ Dogs allowed (on the beach)

Facilities: Three toilet blocks, all recently refurbished are kept very clean and provide washbasins in cubicles and roomy showers (token from reception € 0.65-0.85). Good facilities for disabled visitors and babies. Fully equipped laundry. Motorcaravan service point. Shop stocks essentials (25/5-22/9, limited hours low season). Simple takeaway dishes (1/7-31/8). Good play area (on sand). Games room. Splendid beach with good bathing (best at high tide), fishing, windsurfing and other watersports. Long leads needed in places. Torch useful. Free internet and WiFi. Off site: Pizzeria next door. Tennis. Sailing club 3 km. Riding 7 km. Golf 30 km. Miles of superb coastal walks.

Open: 28 April - 30 September.

Directions: Landéda is 55 km. west of Roscoff via D10 to Plougerneau then D13 crossing river bridge (Aber Wrac'h) and turning west to Lannilis. From N12 Morlaix-Brest road turn north on D59 to Lannilis. Take road to Landéda and then signs for Dunes de Ste Marguerite, 'camping' and des Abers. GPS: 48.59306, -4.60305

Charges guide

Per person	€ 2,72 - € 3,40
child (1-7 yrs)	€ 1,52 - € 1,90
pitch incl. electricity	€ 6,80 - € 8,50

Camping de la Plage

20 rue du Poulquer, F-29950 Bénodet (Finistère)
t: **02 98 57 00 55** e: **info@campingdelaplagebenodet.com**
alanrogers.com/FR29500 www.campingdelaplagebenodet.com

Accommodation: ☑Pitch ☑Mobile home/chalet ☐Hotel/B&B ☐Apartment

This is a large well organised site that has a rural feel, although it is only 300 m. from the beach and 800 m. from the popular seaside town of Bénodet. It has a very short season for touring. There is a great variety of shrubs and trees offering ample shade and privacy for the 300 grassy pitches. There are 190 for touring (electricity 6/10A), all attractively and informally laid out on one side of the site. Access for large units may be difficult. A further 100 pitches are used for mobile homes to rent over a longer season. A splendid pool complex has a retractable cover, flumes, a toboggan and a jacuzzi. Most of the organised entertainment takes place in the bar and on a traditional style terrace. A short walk away are the beach and promenade of Bénodet with shops, bars, restaurants and the mouth of the river Odet. There are organised river trips to the town of Quimper and to the islands in the bay.

Special offers
5% discount for 2 weeks' stay or 10% discount for 4 weeks' stay for touring caravans, mobile home or chalet rentals.

You might like to know
A very nice campsite in Benodet (300 m. from the seafront and 800 m. from Benodet town centre). Ideal for families; kids' club; good aquatic complex with heated covered swimming pool.

☐ Beach on site
☑ **Beach within 1 km.**

☑ **Sandy beach**
☐ Blue Flag quality
☑ **Lifeguard** (high season)
☐ Sun lounger/deckchair hire
☑ **Watersports**
   (e.g. sailing, windsurfing)
☑ **Snacks and drinks**
☐ Sunshades
☐ **Dogs allowed** (on the beach)

Facilities: Four large adequate toilet blocks with facilities for campers with disabilities although access is not easy. Motorcaravan services. Shop (1/7-31/8). Bar with TV and takeaway (1/7-31/8). Heated swimming and paddling pools (one can be covered), flumes, toboggan, jacuzzi (1/5-30/9)). Multisport court. Boules. Exercise bikes. Good play areas. Games room. Internet access. Miniclub and entertainment (July/Aug). Bicycle hire. Mobile homes and chalets for rent (26/4-30/9). Off site: Beach 300 m. Seaside resort of Bénodet, bars, restaurants, shop, cinema 800 m. Boat trips. Fishing, golf, riding and bicycle hire 1 km.

Open: 15 June - 15 September (for touring).

Directions: From Fouesnant take D44 west towards Bénodet. After 10 km. take Le Letty road south. Site is well signed.
GPS: 47.86768, -4.09626

Charges guide

Per unit incl. 2 persons and electricity	€ 20,90 - € 14,10
extra person	€ 6,20
child (2-10 yrs)	€ 3,30
dog	€ 2,60

FRANCE – Arcachon

Camping Club Arcachon

5 allée Galaxie, B.P. 46, F-33312 Arcachon Cedex (Gironde)
t: 05 56 83 24 15 e: info@camping-arcachon.com
alanrogers.com/FR33030 www.camping-arcachon.com

Accommodation: ☑Pitch ☑Mobile home/chalet ☐Hotel/B&B ☐Apartment

This campsite enjoys a position well back from the hustle and bustle, where nights are quiet and facilities are of a high standard. The 176 touring pitches are divided into areas for caravans, motorcaravans and tents and are on neatly formed terraces beneath tall pine trees. Most have electricity (6/10A). The site is quite hilly and the narrow roads that wind around it could possibly make it difficult for larger motorcaravans to manoeuvre and find suitable pitches. At night, wardens ensure that security and noise levels are controlled. A 1 km. walk takes you to the town of Arcachon where there are plenty of shops, bars and restaurants. However, the campsite bar, restaurant and takeaway are open at weekends from April to September (daily in July/August) if you prefer to stay on site. Watersports, paragliding, sailing, tennis tournaments, climbing the biggest sand dune in Europe, and not forgetting such gastronomic delights as oysters and mussels, are readily available.

You might like to know
Children's Clubs. Beach games (sand and grass). Cycle track to beach 1 km. Beach accessible for dogs 4 km. Sailing, windsurfing and kite-surfing. Ocean 10 km. Dune du Pyla 12 km.

☐ **Beach on site**

☑ **Beach within 1 km.**

☑ **Sandy beach**

☐ **Blue Flag quality**

☑ **Lifeguard** (high season)

☑ **Sun lounger/deckchair hire**

☑ **Watersports**
  (e.g. sailing, windsurfing)

☑ **Snacks and drinks**

☑ **Sunshades**

☐ **Dogs allowed** (on the beach)

Facilities: Three sanitary blocks with the usual facilities. Motorcaravan services. Washing machine, dryers. Fridge hire. Shop (15/6-15/9). Bar, restaurant, snack bar, takeaway (April-Sept). Swimming pool (1/5-30/9). Bicycle hire. Play area. Games room. Children's club and entertainment for all age groups (1/7-31/8). Barbecues are only permitted in communal areas. Internet access and WiFi. Off site: Beach 1 km. on foot. Arcachon 2-3 km. Riding 1 km. Golf 2 km.

Open: All year (excl. 12 Nov - 12 Dec).

Directions: Approaching Arcachon from Bordeaux on the N250 take exit for 'Hôpital Jean Hameau' (D217). Cross over bypass following signs for hospital, then signs for Abatilles. At next roundabout follow signs for 'Camping'. Take care as the route travels through suburban housing. Follow campsite signs, not satnav. GPS: 44.6513, -1.174083

Charges guide

Per unit incl. 2 persons	€ 13,00 - € 31,00
extra person	€ 4,00 - € 8,00
child (4-10 yrs)	€ 1,00
electricity	€ 3,00 - € 4,00
animal	€ 2,00 - € 4,00

FRANCE – Hourtin-Plage

Airotel Camping la Côte d'Argent

F-33990 Hourtin-Plage (Gironde)
t: 05 56 09 10 25 e: info@cca33.com
alanrogers.com/FR33110 www.cca33.com

Accommodation: ☑Pitch ☑Mobile home/chalet ☑Hotel/B&B ☐ Apartment

Côte d'Argent is a large, well equipped site for leisurely family holidays. It makes an ideal base for walkers and cyclists with over 100 km. of cycle lanes in the area. Hourtin-Plage is a pleasant invigorating resort on the Atlantic coast and a popular location for watersports enthusiasts. The site's top attraction is its pool complex where wooden bridges connect the pools and islands and there are sunbathing and play areas plus an indoor heated pool. The site has 588 touring pitches (all with 10A electricity), not clearly defined, arranged under trees with some on soft sand. Entertainment takes place at the bar near the entrance (until 00.30). Spread over 20 hectares of undulating sand-based terrain and in the midst of a pine forest. There are 48 hardstandings for motorcaravans outside the site, providing a cheap stopover, but with no access to site facilities. The site is well organised and ideal for children.

You might like to know

Lake (4 km) with watersports and fishing. Access from site to network of 100 km. of cycle tracks. Nearby are the Médoc vineyards, the Arcachon Basin and the Gironde Estuary.

- ☐ Beach on site
- ☑ Beach within 1 km.
- ☑ Sandy beach
- ☑ Blue Flag quality
- ☑ Lifeguard *(high season)*
- ☐ Sun lounger/deckchair hire
- ☑ Watersports
  (e.g. sailing, windsurfing)
- ☑ Snacks and drinks
- ☐ Sunshades
- ☑ Dogs allowed *(on the beach)*

Facilities: Very clean sanitary blocks include provision for disabled visitors. Washing machines. Motorcaravan service points. Large supermarket, restaurant, takeaway, pizzeria bar (all 1/6-15/9). Four outdoor pools with slides and flumes (1/6-19/9). Indoor pool (all season). Massage (Institut de Beauté). Tennis. Play areas. Miniclub, organised entertainment in season. Bicycle hire. Internet. ATM. Charcoal barbecues are not permitted. Hotel (12 rooms). Off site: Path to the beach 300 m. Fishing and riding. Golf 30 km.

Open: 12 May - 19 September.

Directions: Turn off D101 Hourtin - Soulac road 3 km. north of Hourtin. Then join D101E signed Hourtin-Plage. Site is 300 m. from the beach. GPS: 45.22297, -1.16465

Charges guide

Per unit incl. 2 persons and electricity	€ 24,00 - € 52,00
extra person	€ 3,00 - € 7,50
child (3-9 yrs)	€ 2,50 - € 6,50
dog	€ 2,00 - € 5,50

FRANCE – Le Porge

Domaine Naturiste la Jenny

F-33680 Le Porge (Gironde)
t: 05 56 26 56 90   e: info@lajenny.fr
alanrogers.com/FR33300   www.lajenny.fr

Accommodation: ☐ Pitch ☑ Mobile home/chalet ☐ Hotel/B&B ☐ Apartment

Pitches at this campsite are exclusively for chalet accommodation. Situated at the heart of Europe's largest forest, yet within walking distance of the Atlantic beaches through the forest, La Jenny is a naturist site providing 750 high quality chalets, of which 450 are let on behalf of the owners. This is an ideal spot for a quiet and peaceful holiday, yet with a great deal on offer for those seeking a more lively stay. With four pools covering an area of 1,000 m², a wide range of sports amenities, including golf, tennis and archery, there is always something to do. There are many activities for children, including a special club in high season, as well as an extensive programme of evening entertainment. The site's 127 hectares stretches along 3 km. of shoreline.

You might like to know
Huge, wild, semi-private naturist beach, with dazzling colours; qualified lifeguards (Australian method). Beach frequented by clients of the Naturist Residential Park (virtual visit of the beach on www.lajenny.fr)

☐ Beach on site
☑ Beach within 1 km.

☑ Sandy beach

☑ Blue Flag quality

☑ Lifeguard *(high season)*

☐ Sun lounger/deckchair hire

☑ Watersports
  (e.g. sailing, windsurfing)

☐ Snacks and drinks

☐ Sunshades

☐ Dogs allowed *(on the beach)*

Facilities: Supermarket, boulangerie and fish shop. Launderette. Restaurant and pizzeria. Bar and brasserie. Heated pool complex. Hairdresser. Newsagent. Body care centre. Fitness centre. Sauna. Yoga and aquagym. Children's club. Tennis (10 full courts, 4 half courts) with lessons. Short golf course with lessons and clubhouse. Archery. Bicycle hire. Pony club. Diving and instruction courses. Fully fenced, staffed and gated play area (over 3 yrs). WiFi. Off site: Fishing and watersports 300 m. Riding 4 km.

Open: 15 May - 11 September.

Directions: From the Bordeaux ring road take exit 8 signed Lacanau. Follow D107 to Lacanau via Le Temple and La Porge, then towards Lège/Cap Ferret on the D3 to La Jenny (on the right). GPS: 44.84433, -1.21098

Charges guide

Contact the site for details.

Yelloh! Village le Sérignan-Plage

Le Sérignan Plage, F-34410 Sérignan-Plage (Hérault)
t: 04 67 32 35 33   e: info@leserignanplage.com
alanrogers.com/FR34070   www.leserignanplage.com

Accommodation: ☑ Pitch ☑ Mobile home/chalet ☐ Hotel/B&B ☐ Apartment

With direct access onto a superb 600 m. sandy beach (including a naturist section) and with several swimming pools, this is a must for a Mediterranean holiday. It is a friendly, family orientated site with perhaps the most comprehensive range of amenities we have come across. A collection of spa pools (balnéo) built in Romanesque style with colourful terracing and columns, overlooked by a very smart restaurant 'Le Villa' is the 'pièce de résistance'. The balnéo spa is shared with the adjoining naturist site (under the same ownership). There are now over 1,000 pitches with 400 for touring units and this is now a pretty large campsite. The touring pitches vary in size and in terms of shade. They are mainly on sandy soil and all have electricity. There are over 300 mobile homes and chalets to let, plus some 400 privately owned units. The heart of the site developed in the local Catalonian style is some distance from reception and is a busy and informal area with shops, another good restaurant, the Au Pas d'Oc, an indoor pool and a super roof-top bar. There is a range of entertainment for adults and children in the evenings.

Special offers
Sunshine guarantee. In April, May and September, if the weather is poorer than expected, you can rearrange, shorten or cancel your holidays for no cost. You will only pay for nights actually spent on site.

You might like to know
Yelloh! Village Le Serignan Plage has a brilliant aqua complex with a lagoon style pool covering 850 sq.m, and a special covered pool for very young swimmers.

☑ Beach on site
☐ Beach within 1 km.

☑ Sandy beach

☑ Blue Flag quality

☑ Lifeguard *(high season)*

☑ Sun lounger/deckchair hire

☐ Watersports
  (e.g. sailing, windsurfing)

☑ Snacks and drinks

☑ Sunshades

☐ Dogs allowed *(on the beach)*

Facilities: Several modern blocks of individual design with good facilities including showers with washbasin and WC. Facilities for disabled people. Baby bathroom. Launderette. Motorcaravan services. Supermarket, bakery and newsagent (all season). Other shops (1/6-15/9). ATM. Restaurants, bar and takeaway. Hairdresser. Balnéo spa. Gym. Heated indoor pool. Outdoor pools (24/4-21/9). Children's clubs. Evening entertainment. Sporting activities. Bicycle hire. Bus to Sérignan village July/Aug. Beach (lifeguards 1/6-15/9). Off site: Riding 2 km. Golf 10 km. Sailing and windsurfing school on beach (lifeguard in high season). Local markets.

Open: 29 April - 20 September.

Directions: From A9 exit 35 (Béziers Est) follow signs for Sérignan, D64 (9 km). Before Sérignan, turn left, Sérignan-Plage (4 km). At small sign (blue) turn right. At T-junction turn left over small road bridge and after left hand bend. Site is 100 m. GPS: 43.26398, 3.321

Charges guide

Per unit incl. 2 persons and electricity	€ 15,00 - € 48,00
extra person	€ 5,00 - € 8,00
child (3-7 yrs)	free - € 8,00
dog	€ 4,00

FRANCE – Marseillan-Plage

Camping la Creole

74 avenue des campings, F-34340 Marseillan-Plage (Hérault)
t: 04 67 21 92 69 e: campinglacreole@wanadoo.fr
alanrogers.com/FR34220 www.campinglacreole.com

Accommodation: ☑Pitch ☑Mobile home/chalet ☐ Hotel/B&B ☐ Apartment

This is a surprisingly tranquil, well cared for, small campsite in the middle of this bustling resort that will appeal to those seeking a rather less frenetic ambience typical of many sites in this area. Essentially a family orientated site, it offers around 110 good-sized, level grass pitches, all with 6A electricity and mostly with shade from trees and shrubs. It also benefits from direct access to an extensive sandy beach and the fact that there is no swimming pool or bar actually contributes to the tranquillity. It may even be seen as an advantage for families with younger children. The beach will be the main attraction here no doubt, and the town's extensive range of bars, restaurants and shops are all within a couple of minutes walk.

You might like to know
Gently sloping beach of fine sand where children can swim in total security. Plenty of shade on the campsite. All shops and services less than 100 m. from the site.

☑ Beach on site
☐ Beach within 1 km.
☑ Sandy beach
☑ Blue Flag quality
☑ Lifeguard *(high season)*
☐ Sun lounger/deckchair hire
☑ Watersports
   (e.g. sailing, windsurfing)
☑ Snacks and drinks
☐ Sunshades
☐ Dogs allowed *(on the beach)*

Facilities: Toilet facilities are housed in a traditional building, modernised inside to provide perfectly adequate, if not particularly luxurious facilities including some washbasins in private cabins, a baby room and dog shower. Small play area. In high season beach games, dances, sangria evenings etc, are organised, all aimed particularly towards families. Barbecue area. Bicycle hire. Off site: Local market day Tuesday. Riding 1 km.

Open: 1 April - 15 October.

Directions: From A9 exit 34 take N312 towards Agde, then the N112 towards Sète keeping a look-out for signs to Marseillan-Plage off this road. Site is well signed in Marseillan-Plage. GPS: 43.3206, 3.5501

Charges guide

Per unit incl. 2 persons	€ 13,50 - € 27,20
extra person	€ 3,00 - € 5,00
electricity	€ 2,80
dog	€ 2,00 - € 3,00

Yelloh! Village Mer et Soleil

Chemin de Notre Dame á Saint Martin, Rochelongue, F-34300 Cap d'Agde (Hérault)
t: 04 67 94 21 14 e: contact@camping-mer-soleil.com
alanrogers.com/FR34290 www.camping-mer-soleil.com

Accommodation: ☑Pitch ☑Mobile home/chalet ☐Hotel/B&B ☐Apartment

Close to Cap d'Agde, this is a popular, well equipped site with many facilities. The pool area is particularly attractive with large palm trees, a whirlpool and slides and a gym and wellness centre. An upstairs restaurant overlooks this area and the entertainment stage next to it. All ages are catered for and evening entertainment in July and August includes live shows. There are 500 pitches, around half taken by mobile homes and chalets (some to let, some privately owned). The touring pitches are hedged and have good shade, all with 6A electricity. From the back of the site, a 1 km. long path leads to the white sandy beach at Rochelongue. The attractively designed balnéo spa and wellness centre includes saunas, pools and jacuzzis. Professional staff offer a wide range of massages and beauty treatments.

You might like to know

Plage Rochelongue is the nearest beach, about 1 km. away. Nearby are the popular resort of Cap d'Agde, the Camargue, the Canal du Midi and the vineyards of Languedoc Rousillon.

☐ Beach on site
☑ Beach within 1 km.

☑ Sandy beach

☐ Blue Flag quality

☑ Lifeguard *(high season)*

☑ Sun lounger/deckchair hire

☑ Watersports
  (e.g. sailing, windsurfing)

☑ Snacks and drinks

☑ Sunshades

☐ Dogs allowed *(on the beach)*

Facilities: One large toilet block plus three smaller ones are fully equipped. Attractive units for children with small toilets, etc. Units for disabled visitors. Motorcaravan service point. Washing machine. Shop. Bar and restaurant. Swimming pools. Gym. Tennis. Archery. Sporting activities and evening entertainment. Off site: Beach 1 km. Riding 1 km. Sports complex opposite site.

Open: 3 April - 16 October.

Directions: From A9 exit 34, follow N312 for Agde. It joins the N112 Béziers - Sète road. Cross bridge over Hérault river and turn right for Rochelongue. Turn left at next roundabout and site is a little further on the right.
GPS: 43.286183, 3.478

Charges guide

Per unit incl. 2 persons and electricity	€ 36,00
extra person	€ 5,00
child (7-13 yrs)	€ 4,50
dog	€ 4,00

FRANCE – Portiragnes-Plage

Camping les Sablons

Avenue des Muriers, F-34420 Portiragnes-Plage (Hérault)
t: 04 67 90 90 55   e: contact@les-sablons.com
alanrogers.com/FR34400   www.les-sablons.com

Accommodation: ☑Pitch ☑Mobile home/chalet ☐ Hotel/B&B ☐ Apartment

Les Sablons is an impressive and popular site with lots going on. Most of the facilities are arranged around the entrance with shops, a restaurant, bar and a large pool complex with no less than five slides, three heated pools and a large stage for entertainment. There is also direct access to the white sandy beach at the back of the site close to a small lake. There is good shade on the majority of the site, although some of the newer touring pitches have less shade but are nearer the gate to the beach. On level sandy grass, all have 6A electricity. Of around 800 pitches, around half are taken by a range of mobile homes and chalets (many for hire, some by British tour operators). A wide range of sporting activities, and evening entertainment is arranged with much for children to do. In fact, this is a real holiday venue aiming to keep all the family happy.

You might like to know
The site has direct access to the beach and dunes (closed 23.00-07.00). There is also a lake with hides for bird watching.

☑ Beach on site

☐ Beach within 1 km.

☑ Sandy beach

☑ Blue Flag quality

☐ Lifeguard *(high season)*

☐ Sun lounger/deckchair hire

☑ Watersports
  (e.g. sailing, windsurfing)

☐ Snacks and drinks

☐ Sunshades

☐ Dogs allowed *(on the beach)*

Facilities: Well equipped, modernised toilet blocks include large showers, some with washbasins. Baby baths and facilities for disabled visitors. Supermarket, bakery and newsagent. Restaurant, bar and takeaway. Swimming pool complex. Entertainment and activity programme with sports, music and cultural activities. Beach club. Tennis. Archery. Play areas. Electronic games. ATM. Internet access. Off site: Riding 200 m. Bicycle hire 100 m.

Open: 1 April - 30 September.

Directions: From A9 exit 35 (Béziers Est) follow signs for Vias and Agde (N112). After large roundabout pass exit to Cers then take exit for Portiragnes (D37). Follow for about 5 km. and pass over Canal du Midi towards Portiragnes-Plage. Site is on left after roundabout. GPS: 43.28003, 3.36396

Charges guide

Per unit incl. 2 persons and electricity	€ 18,00 - € 46,00
extra person	€ 6,00 - € 10,00
child (5-13 yrs)	free - € 8,00
dog	€ 4,00

FRANCE – Vielle-Saint-Girons

Camping Club International Eurosol

Route de la Plage, F-40560 Vielle-Saint-Girons (Landes)
t: 05 58 47 90 14 e: contact@camping-eurosol.com
alanrogers.com/FR40060 www.camping-eurosol.com

Accommodation: ☑Pitch ☑Mobile home/chalet ☐Hotel/B&B ☐Apartment

Eurosol is an attractive and well maintained site extending over 15 hectares of undulating ground amongst mature pine trees giving good shade. Of the 356 pitches, 209 have electricity (10A) with 120 fully serviced. A wide range of mobile homes and chalets are available for rent too. This is very much a family site with multilingual entertainers. Many games and tournaments are organised and a beach volleyball competition is held each evening in front of the bar. The adjacent boules terrain is also floodlit. An excellent sandy beach 700 metres from the site has supervised bathing in high season, and is ideal for surfing. The landscaped swimming pool complex is impressive with three large pools, one of which is covered and heated, and a large children's paddling pool. There is a convivial restaurant and takeaway food service. A large supermarket is well stocked with fresh bread daily and international newspapers. A number of cycle trails lead from the site through the vast forests of Les Landes, and a riding centre is located just 100 m. from Eurosol.

You might like to know

A quiet and very high quality camping village in the shade of the pine forest - a great spot for unforgettable family holidays.

☐ Beach on site
☑ Beach within 1 km.
☑ Sandy beach
☐ Blue Flag quality
☑ Lifeguard *(high season)*
☐ Sun lounger/deckchair hire
☐ Watersports
   (e.g. sailing, windsurfing)
☑ Snacks and drinks
☐ Sunshades
☑ Dogs allowed *(on the beach)*

Facilities: Four main toilet blocks and two smaller blocks are comfortable and clean with facilities for babies and disabled visitors. Motorcaravan services. Fridge rental. Well stocked shop and bar (all season). Restaurant, takeaway (10/6-4/9). Stage for live shows arranged in July/Aug. Outdoor swimming pool and heated covered pool (all season). Tennis. Multisport court. Bicycle hire. Internet and WiFi. Charcoal barbecues are not permitted. Off site: Riding school opposite. Fishing 700 m. Golf 18 km.

Open: 15 May - 11 September.

Directions: Turn off D652 at St Girons on the D42 towards St Girons-Plage. Site is on left before coming to beach (4.5 km).
GPS: 43.95166, -1.35212

Charges guide

Per unit incl. 2 persons and electricity	€ 18,00 - € 35,00
extra person (over 4 yrs)	€ 5,00
dog	€ 4,00

FRANCE – Mimizan-Plage

Airotel Club Marina-Landes

Rue Marina, F-40200 Mimizan (Landes)
t: 05 58 09 12 66 e: contact@clubmarina.com
alanrogers.com/FR40080 www.marinalandes.com

Accommodation: ☑Pitch ☑Mobile home/chalet ☐Hotel/B&B ☐Apartment

Well maintained and clean, with helpful staff, Club Marina-Landes would be a very good choice for a family holiday. Activities include discos, play groups for children, specially trained staff to entertain teenagers and concerts for more mature campers. There are numerous sports opportunities and a superb sandy beach nearby. A nightly curfew ensures that all have a good night's sleep. The site has 444 touring pitches (304 with 10A electricity) and 128 mobile homes and chalets for rent. The pitches are on firm grass, most with hedges and they are large (mostly 100 m² or larger). If ever a campsite could be said to have two separate identities, then Club Marina-Landes is surely the one. In early and late season it is quiet, with the pace of life in low gear – come July and until 1 September, all the facilities are open and there is fun for all the family with the chance that family members will only meet together at meal times.

You might like to know
Why not take the Mailloueyre lake trail (1 km. – 15 minutes on foot)? The area is officially classified as a Nature Reserve – a delight for botanists and all nature lovers.

☐ Beach on site
☑ Beach within 1 km.
☑ Sandy beach
☐ Blue Flag quality
☑ Lifeguard *(high season)*
☐ Sun lounger/deckchair hire
☑ Watersports
  (e.g. sailing, windsurfing)
☑ Snacks and drinks
☐ Sunshades
☑ Dogs allowed *(on the beach)*

Facilities: Five toilet blocks (opened as required), well maintained with showers and many washbasins in cabins. Facilities for babies, children and disabled visitors. Laundry facilities. Motorcaravan services. Fridge hire. Shop (freshly baked bread) and bar (30/4-10/9). Restaurant, snack bar, pizzas and takeaway (1/5-10/9). Covered pool and outdoor pools (30/4-13/9). Minigolf. Tennis. Bicycle hire. Play area. Internet access. Entertainment and activities (high season). Gas or electric barbecues only.
Off site: Beach and fishing 500 m. Bus service 1 km. Riding 1 km. Golf 8 km. Mimizan 8 km.

Open: 30 April - 13 September.

Directions: Heading west from Mimizan centre, take D626 passing Abbey Museum. Straight on at lights (crossing D87/D67). Next lights turn left. After 2 km. at T-junction turn left. Follow signs to site. GPS: 44.20447, -1.29099

Charges guide

Per unit incl. 2 persons and electricity	€ 17,00 - € 44,00
extra person (+13)	€ 3,00 - € 8,00
child (3-13 yrs)	€ 3,00 - € 6,00
dog	€ 2,00 - € 4,00

FRANCE – Biscarrosse

Camping du Domaine de la Rive

Route de Bordeaux, F-40600 Biscarrosse (Landes)
t: 05 58 78 12 33 e: info@camping-de-la-rive.fr
alanrogers.com/FR40100 www.larive.fr

Accommodation: ☑Pitch ☑Mobile home/chalet ☐Hotel/B&B ☐Apartment

Surrounded by pine woods, La Rive has a superb beach-side location on Lac de Sanguinet. It provides mostly level, numbered and clearly defined pitches of 100 m² all with electricity connections (6A). The swimming pool complex is wonderful with pools linked by water channels and bridges. There is also a jacuzzi, paddling pool and two large swimming pools all surrounded by sunbathing areas and decorated with palm trees. An indoor pool is heated and open all season. There may be some aircraft noise from a nearby army base. This is a friendly site with a good mix of nationalities. The latest addition is a super children's aquapark with various games. The beach is excellent, shelving gently to provide safe bathing for all ages. There are windsurfers and small craft can be launched from the site's slipway.

You might like to know
This lakeside beach offers many watersports including catamaran sailing, rowing and canoeing and in the afternoons from Monday to Thursday, jet skis.

☑ Beach on site
☐ Beach within 1 km.
☑ Sandy beach
☐ Blue Flag quality
☐ Lifeguard *(high season)*
☐ Sun lounger/deckchair hire
☑ Watersports
   (e.g. sailing, windsurfing)
☐ Snacks and drinks
☐ Sunshades
☐ Dogs allowed *(on the beach)*

Facilities: Five good clean toilet blocks have washbasins in cabins and mainly British style toilets. Facilities for disabled visitors. Baby baths. Motorcaravan service point. Shop with gas. Restaurant. Bar serving snacks and takeaway. Swimming pool complex (supervised July/Aug). Games room. Play area. Tennis. Bicycle hire. Boules. Archery. Fishing. Waterskiing. Watersports equipment hire. Tournaments (June-Aug). Skateboard park. Trampolines. Miniclub. No charcoal barbecues on pitches. Off site: Golf 8 km. Riding 5 km.

Open: 3 April - 5 September.

Directions: Take D652 from Sanguinet to Biscarrosse and site is signed on the right in about 6 km. Turn right and follow tarmac road for 2 km. GPS: 44.46052, -1.13065

Charges guide

Per unit incl. 2 persons and electricity	€ 21,50 - € 46,00
extra person	€ 3,60 - € 7,80
child (3-7 yrs)	€ 2,40 - € 6,30
dog	€ 2,10 - € 5,00

FRANCE – Messanges

Camping le Vieux Port

Plage Sud, F-40660 Messanges (Landes)
t: 01 76 76 70 00 e: contact@levieuxport.com
alanrogers.com/FR40180 www.levieuxport.com

Accommodation: ☑Pitch ☑Mobile home/chalet ☐Hotel/B&B ☐Apartment

A well established destination appealing particularly to families with teenage children, this lively site has 1,546 pitches of mixed size, most with electricity (6A) and some fully serviced. The camping area is well shaded by pines and pitches are generally of a good size, attractively grouped around the toilet blocks. There are many tour operators here and well over a third of the site is taken up with mobile homes and another 400 pitches are used for tents. An enormous 7,000 m² Aquatic Parc is now open. The heated pool complex is exceptional, boasting five outdoor pools and three large water slides. There is also a heated indoor pool. The area to the north of Bayonne is heavily forested and a number of very large campsites are attractively located close to the superb Atlantic beaches. Le Vieux Port is probably the largest, and certainly one of the most impressive, of these. At the back of the site a path leads across the dunes to a good beach (500 m). A little train also trundles to the beach on a fairly regular basis in high season (small charge). All in all, this is a lively site with a great deal to offer an active family.

Special offers
Special offers on accommodation rentals.

You might like to know
Discover the varied local gastronomy. Le Vieux Port is very close to both the Basque Country and Spain (only 70 km. away).

☑ Beach on site
☐ Beach within 1 km.

☑ Sandy beach
☐ Blue Flag quality
☑ Lifeguard *(high season)*
☐ Sun lounger/deckchair hire
☑ Watersports
   (e.g. sailing, windsurfing)
☑ Snacks and drinks
☑ Sunshades
☑ Dogs allowed *(on the beach)*

Facilities: Nine well appointed, recently renovated toilet blocks with facilities for disabled people. Motorcaravan services. Good supermarket and various smaller shops in high season. Several restaurants, takeaway and three bars (all open all season). Large pool complex (no Bermuda shorts) including new covered pool and Polynesian themed bar. Tennis. Multisport pitch. Minigolf. Bicycle hire. Riding centre. Organised activities in high season including frequent discos and karaoke evenings. Only communal barbecues are allowed.
Off site: Fishing 1 km. Golf 8 km.

Open: 31 March - 26 September.

Directions: Leave RN10 at Magescq exit heading for Soustons. Pass through Soustons following signs for Vieux-Boucau. Bypass this town and site is clearly signed to the left at second roundabout. GPS: 43.79778, -1.40111

Charges guide

Per unit incl. 2 persons and electricity	€ 19,00 - € 54,30
extra person	€ 4,50 - € 8,30
child (under 13 yrs)	€ 3,50 - € 5,70
dog	€ 3,00 - € 5,20

FRANCE – Moliets-Plage

Le Saint-Martin Camping

Avenue de l'Océan, F-40660 Moliets-Plage (Landes)
t: 05 58 48 52 30 e: contact@camping-saint-martin.fr
alanrogers.com/FR40190 www.camping-saint-martin.fr

Accommodation: ☑Pitch ☑Mobile home/chalet ☐Hotel/B&B ☐Apartment

A family site aimed mainly at couples and young families, Saint-Martin is a welcome change from most of the sites in this area in that it has only a small number of chalets (85) compared to the number of touring pitches (575). First impressions are of a neat, tidy, well cared for site and the direct access to a wonderful fine sandy beach is an added bonus. The pitches are mainly typically French in style with low hedges separating them and with some shade. Electricity hook ups are 10-15A and a number of pitches also have water and drainage. Entertainment in high season is low key (with the emphasis on quiet nights) – daytime competitions and a miniclub, plus the occasional evening entertainment, well away from the pitches and with no discos or karaoke. With pleasant chalets and mobile homes to rent, and an 18-hole golf course 700 m. away (special rates have been negotiated), this would be an ideal destination for a golfing weekend or longer stay.

You might like to know
Hutchets stream, a conservation area, is delightful with a number of walks and some beautiful views.

☑ Beach on site
☐ Beach within 1 km.

☑ Sandy beach
☑ Blue Flag quality
☑ Lifeguard *(high season)*
☐ Sun lounger/deckchair hire
☑ Watersports
   (e.g. sailing, windsurfing)
☐ Snacks and drinks
☐ Sunshades
☑ Dogs allowed *(on the beach)*

Facilities: Seven toilet blocks of a high standard and very well maintained, have washbasins in cabins, large showers, baby rooms and facilities for disabled visitors. Motorcaravan service point. Washing machines and dryers. Fridge rental. Supermarket. Bars, restaurants and takeaways. Indoor pool, jacuzzi and sauna (charged July/Aug). Outdoor pool area with jacuzzi and paddling pool (15/6-15/9). Multisport pitch. Play area. Beach access. Internet access. Electric barbecues only. Off site: Excellent area for cycling, bicycle hire 500 m. Golf and tennis 700 m. Riding 8 km.

Open: 19 March - 11 November.

Directions: From the N10 take D142 to Lèon, then D652 to Moliets-et-Mar. Follow signs to Moliets-Plage, site is well signed.
GPS: 43.85242, -1.38732

Charges guide

Per unit incl. 2 persons and electricity	€ 22,00 - € 44,50
extra person	€ 6,00 - € 7,00
child (under 10 yrs)	€ 4,00 - € 5,00
dog	free - € 4,00

Prices are for reserved pitches.

Camping le Dolmen

58 chemin de Beaumer, F-56340 Carnac (Morbihan)
t: 02 97 52 12 35 e: contact@campingledolmen.com
alanrogers.com/56510 www.campingledolmen.com

Accommodation: ☑Pitch ☑Mobile home/chalet ☐Hotel/B&B ☐Apartment

Le Dolmen is a family site located on the eastern edge of Carnac. The site has 130 pitches, of which around 70 are available to tourers. Other pitches are taken by mobile homes (around 12 are to rent). Pitches are of a good size and are mostly equipped with electricity. A number of pitches have been specially equipped for motor caravans (with services). On-site amenities include a snack bar and a swimming pool. The nearest beach, Le Men Dû, is around 600 m. away. This is a particularly attractive beach, shelving gently and with crystal waters. Carnac needs little introduction and is best known for its alignments of more than 3,000 prehistoric standing stones. Carnac-Plage, in high season, is quite different from the old town, with many lively bars and night clubs. To the east, La Trinité-sur-Mer is one of Brittany's premier sailing resorts and has many attractive restaurants. To the south, Quiberon retains a character all of its own with an important fishing tradition, particularly for sardines.

You might like to know

Children's Club on site. Marina and Yacht Club in Carnac. Near Quiberon with sailings to Belle Ile en Mer. Rugged coastline for lovers of the seashore.

☐ Beach on site

☑ Beach within 1 km.

☑ Sandy beach

☐ Blue Flag quality

☑ Lifeguard *(high season)*

☐ Sun lounger/deckchair hire

☐ Watersports
  (e.g. sailing, windsurfing)

☑ Snacks and drinks

☑ Sunshades

☑ Dogs allowed *(on the beach)*

Facilities: Snack bar. Morning bread service. Swimming pool. Play area. Volleyball. Activity and entertainment programme. Tourist information. Motorcaravan services. Mobile homes for rent. Off site: Nearest beach 600 m. Fishing. Golf 800 m. Sailing 1 km.

Open: 1 April - 11 September.

Directions: Approaching from the north (Auray) take D768 towards Quiberon and then D119 to Carnac. Upon arriving in Carnac, follow signs to Carnac Plage and then to La Trinité-sur-Mer using D186 (Avenue des Druides). The site is clearly indicated to the left, on the edge of the town. GPS: 47.58076, -3.05751

Charges guide

Per unit incl. 2 persons and electricity	€ 20,00 - € 31,00

FRANCE – Bidart

Camping le Pavillon Royal

Avenue du Prince de Galles, F-64210 Bidart (Pyrénées-Atlantiques)
t: 05 59 23 00 54 e: info@pavillon-royal.com
alanrogers.com/FR64060 www.pavillon-royal.com

Accommodation: ☑Pitch ☑Mobile home/chalet ☐Hotel/B&B ☐Apartment

Le Pavillon Royal has an excellent situation on raised ground overlooking the sea, with good views along the coast to the south and to the north coast of Spain beyond. There is a large heated swimming pool and sunbathing area in the centre of the site. The camping area is divided up into 303 marked, level pitches, many of a good size. About 50 are reserved for tents and are only accessible on foot. The remainder are connected by asphalt roads. All have electricity and most are fully serviced. Much of the campsite is in full sun, although the area for tents is shaded. Beneath the site – and only a very short walk down – stretches a wide sandy beach where the Atlantic rollers provide ideal conditions for surfing. A central, marked-out section of the beach is supervised by lifeguards (from mid June). There is also a section with rocks and pools. Reservation for this site in high season is advisable.

You might like to know
Free fitness suite and access to wellness centre. Pool heated by solar power. Free WiFi access.

- ☑ **Beach on site**
- ☐ **Beach within 1 km.**
- ☑ **Sandy beach**
- ☐ **Blue Flag quality**
- ☑ **Lifeguard** (high season)
- ☐ **Sun lounger/deckchair hire**
- ☑ **Watersports**
  (e.g. sailing, windsurfing)
- ☑ **Snacks and drinks**
- ☐ **Sunshades**
- ☐ **Dogs allowed** (on the beach)

Facilities: Good quality toilet blocks with baby baths and unit for disabled people. Washing facilities are closed at night except for two single night units. Washing machines, dryers. Motorcaravan services. Shop (including gas). Restaurant and takeaway (from 1/6). Bar (all season). Heated swimming and paddling pools. Playground. General room, TV room, games room, films. Fishing. Surf school. Dogs are not accepted. Fitness room. Off site: Golf 500 m. Bicycle hire 2 km. Riding 3 km. Sailing 5 km.

Open: 15 May - 30 September.

Directions: From A63 exit 4, take the N10 south towards Bidart. At roundabout after the 'Intermarché' supermarket turn right (signed for Biarritz). After 600 m. turn left at site sign. GPS: 43.45458, -1.57649

Charges guide

Per unit incl. 2 persons, electricity and water	€ 29,00 - € 49,00
tent incl. 1 or 2 persons	€ 23,00 - € 39,00
extra person (over 4 yrs)	€ 7,50 - € 10,00

FRANCE – Saint Jean-de-Luz

Camping les Tamaris Plage

Quartier Acotz, 720 route des Plages, F-64500 Saint Jean-de-Luz (Pyrénées-Atlantiques)
t: 05 59 26 55 90   e: tamaris1@wanadoo.fr
alanrogers.com/FR64080   www.tamaris-plage.com

Accommodation: ☑Pitch ☑Mobile home/chalet ☐ Hotel/B&B ☐ Apartment

This is a popular, small and pleasant site which is well kept. It is situated outside the town and just across the road from a sandy beach. The 35 touring pitches, all with 7/10A electricity, are of good size and separated by hedges, on slightly sloping ground with some shade. The site becomes full for July and August with families on long stays, so reservation then is essential. Mobile homes for rent occupy a further 40 pitches. A leisure centre and club provide a heated pool and various other free facilities for adults and children. A gym, Turkish bath, massage and other relaxing amenities are available at an extra charge. There is no shop, but bread is available daily from across the road. Opposite the site, a popular surf school offers instruction to new and experienced surfers from the sandy Mayarco beach.

You might like to know
Activities from this sandy beach include canoeing, kayaking, scuba diving, open sea fishing and sea trips. There is also an attractive coastal walk.

☑ Beach on site
☐ Beach within 1 km.

☑ Sandy beach
☑ Blue Flag quality
☑ Lifeguard *(high season)*
☐ Sun lounger/deckchair hire
☑ Watersports
   (e.g. sailing, windsurfing)
☐ Snacks and drinks
☐ Sunshades
☐ Dogs allowed *(on the beach)*

Facilities: The single toilet block of good quality and unusual design should be an ample provision. Facilities for disabled people. Washing machine. Wellness health club with free facilities: swimming pool, TV and play room, a club for children (4-11 yrs); and on payment: gym, Turkish bath and other spa facilities. Sunbathing area, jacuzzi, adult TV lounge. Off site: Beach, fishing, surfing (with instruction) 30 m. Bicycle hire and golf 4 km. Riding 7 km.

Open: All year.

Directions: Proceed south on N10 and 1.5 km. after Guethary take first road on right (before access to the motorway and Carrefour centre commercial) and follow site signs.
GPS: 43.41794, -1.62399

Charges guide

Per unit incl. 2 persons and electricity	€ 17,00 - € 29,00
extra person (over 2 yrs)	€ 5,00 - € 7,00
dog	€ 6,00

FRANCE – Argelès-sur-Mer

Camping le Littoral

Route du Littoral, F-66700 Argelès-sur-Mer (Pyrénées-Orientales)
t: 04 68 81 17 74   e: infos@camping-le-littoral.fr
alanrogers.com/FR66060   www.camping-le-littoral.fr

Accommodation: ☑Pitch ☑Mobile home/chalet ☐Hotel/B&B ☐Apartment

Sites with access to the beach are difficult to find and, even though Le Littoral is not directly beside the beach, it is only 800 metres away by footpath. It offers much accommodation in mobile homes as well as 20 good sized, level touring pitches with shade and 15A electricity. An attractive pool area is open from May to September. Argelès is a very popular holiday resort with good sandy beaches. The border with Spain is only 30 km. The site is situated on the north side of Argelès between the coast road and the beach, so access is good, although there could be some road noise in high season. The site has been taken over by a new group, Camp'Atlantic and is looking smart with a new reception and tarmac roadways. However, there are now fewer touring pitches and the emphasis is on mobile homes with over 127 to let and 105 privately owned. The site is well looked after and the pool area is particularly welcoming.

You might like to know
Experience the musical festival 'les Déferlantes' at Argelès-sur-Mer or the 'Fètes de la Saint Vincent' at Collioure. Visit the Abbey at Saint Martin du Canigou.

☑ **Beach on site**
☐ **Beach within 1 km.**
☑ **Sandy beach**
☑ **Blue Flag quality**
☐ **Lifeguard** *(high season)*
☐ **Sun lounger/deckchair hire**
☐ **Watersports**
   (e.g. sailing, windsurfing)
☐ **Snacks and drinks**
☐ **Sunshades**
☐ **Dogs allowed** *(on the beach)*

Facilities: Large modern toilet block, fully equipped and with some washbasins in cabins. Baby bath. Some facilities for disabled visitors. Washing machines. Shop. Bar, restaurant and takeaway (15/6-15/9). Heated swimming pool (May-Sept). Entertainment in high season. Play area. Bicycle hire. Internet. Path to beach. Communal barbecues only. Off site: Tourist train in high season. Within walking distance aquatic park, adventure park, karting, riding and minigolf.

Open: 5 April - 14 September.

Directions: From A9 take exit 42 (Perpignan-Sud) and follow N114 for Argelès. At exit 10 follow directions for Taxo d'Avall then Plage Nord. Site is clearly signed off the coast road in the St Cyprien direction.
GPS: 42.580585, 3.032948

Charges guide

Per unit incl. 2 persons and electricity	€ 32,00 - € 44,00
extra person	€ 6,00 - € 9,00
child (4-10 yrs)	€ 4,00 - € 7,00

No credit cards.

Yelloh! Village le Brasilia

B.P. 204, F-66141 Canet-en-Roussillon (Pyrénées-Orientales)
t: **04 68 80 23 82** e: **info@yellohvillage-brasilia.com**
alanrogers.com/FR66070 **www.brasilia.fr**

Accommodation: ☑ Pitch ☑ Mobile home/chalet ☐ Hotel/B&B ☐ Apartment

Situated across the yacht harbour from the upmarket resort of Canet-Plage, le Brasilia is an impressive, well managed family site directly beside the beach. It is pretty, neat and well kept with an amazingly wide range of facilities – indeed, it is camping at its best. There are 473 neatly hedged touring pitches, all with electricity and many with water and drainage. They vary in size from 80-120 m² and some of the longer pitches are suitable for two families together. With a range of shade from pines and flowering shrubs, less on pitches near the beach, there are neat access roads (sometimes narrow for large units). There are also 130 pitches with mobile homes or chalets to rent. The sandy beach here is busy, with a beach club (you can hire windsurfing boards). A new pool complex is planned with pools catering for all ages and hydrotherapy facilities for adults. The village area of the site offers a range of shops, a busy restaurant and bar, entertainment (including a night club) and clubs for children of all ages. A member of Yelloh! Village and Leading Campings groups.

You might like to know
This site has direct access to a nine kilometre beach and nearby harbour of the upmarket resort of Canet-en-Roussillon where kitesurfing, windsurfing, diving and sailing lessons are all available.

☑ **Beach on site**
☐ **Beach within 1 km.**

☑ **Sandy beach**
☑ **Blue Flag quality**
☑ **Lifeguard** *(high season)*
☑ **Sun lounger/deckchair hire**
☑ **Watersports**
   (e.g. sailing, windsurfing)
☑ **Snacks and drinks**
☑ **Sunshades**
☐ **Dogs allowed** *(on the beach)*

Facilities: Ten modern sanitary blocks are very well equipped and maintained, with British style WCs (some Turkish) and washbasins in cabins. Good facilities for children and for disabled people. Laundry. Motorcaravan services. Shops. Gas. Bars and restaurant. Pool complex (heated). Play areas. Tennis. Sporting activities. Library, games and video room. Hairdresser. Internet café and WiFi. Daily entertainment programme. Bicycle hire. Only gas or electric barbecues are allowed. Off site: Boat launchng and sailing 500 m. Riding 5 km. Golf 12 km.

Open: 26 April - 27 September.

Directions: From A9 exit 41 (Perpignan Centre, Rivesaltes) follow signs for Le Barcarès and Canet on D83 for 10 km. then for Canet (D81). At first Canet roundabout, turn fully back on yourself (Sainte-Marie) and watch for the Brasilia sign almost immediately on the right. GPS: 42.70467, 3.03483

Charges guide

Per unit incl. 2 persons and electricity (6A)	€ 19,00 - € 47,50
extra person	€ 6,00 - € 8,50
child (3-6 yrs)	free - € 8,50
dog (max. 2)	€ 4,00

FRANCE – Bormes-les-Mimosas

Camp du Domaine

B.P. 207 La Favière, F-83230 Bormes-les-Mimosas (Var)
t: 04 94 71 03 12 e: mail@campdudomaine.com
alanrogers.com/FR83120 www.campdudomaine.com

Accommodation: ☑Pitch ☑Mobile home/chalet ☐Hotel/B&B ☐Apartment

Camp du Domaine, 3 km. south of Le Lavandou, is a large, attractive beach-side site with 1,200 pitches set in 45 hectares of pinewood, although surprisingly it does not give the impression of being so big. The pitches are large (up to 200 m²) and most are reasonably level, 800 with 10A electricity. The most popular pitches are beside the beach, but the ones furthest away are generally larger and have more shade. Amongst the trees, many are more suitable for tents. The price for all the pitches is the same – smaller but near the beach or larger with shade. The beach is the attraction however and everyone tries to get close. American motorhomes are not accepted. Despite its size, the site does not feel too busy, except perhaps around the supermarket. This is mainly because many pitches are hidden in the trees, the access roads are quite wide and it all covers quite a large area (some of the beach pitches are 600 m. from the entrance). Its popularity makes early reservation necessary over a long season (about mid June to mid Sept) as regular clients book from season to season. English is spoken.

Facilities: Ten modern, well used but clean toilet blocks. Mostly Turkish WCs. Facilities for disabled visitors (but steep steps). Baby room. Washing machines. Fridge hire. Well stocked supermarket, bars, pizzeria (all open all season). No swimming pool. Excellent play area. Boats, pedaloes for hire. Wide range of watersports. Games, competitions (July/Aug). Children's club. Tennis. Multisport courts. Barbecues are strictly forbidden. Dogs are not accepted 4/7-25/8. Off site: Bicycle hire 500 m. Riding or golf 15 km.

Open: 27 March - 31 October.

Directions: Just outside and to west of Le Lavandou, at roundabout, turn off D559 towards the sea on road signed Favière. After 2 km. turn left at site signs. GPS: 43.11779, 6.35176

Charges guide

Per unit incl. 2 persons and electricity	€ 27,00 - € 39,00
extra person	€ 5,60 - € 8,50
child (under 7 yrs)	€ 1,00 - € 4,50

You might like to know

From the beach: all watersports, sailing school and diving school. From Lavandou: boat trips to the Iles d'Or (Port Cros and Porquerolles). Nearby: the Provençal village of Bormes les Mimosas.

☑ **Beach on site**

☐ **Beach within 1 km.**

☑ **Sandy beach**

☐ **Blue Flag quality**

☑ **Lifeguard** *(high season)*

☑ **Sun lounger/deckchair hire**

☑ **Watersports**
   (e.g. sailing, windsurfing)

☐ **Snacks and drinks**

☑ **Sunshades**

☐ **Dogs allowed** *(on the beach)*

FRANCE – Longeville-sur-Mer

Camping le Petit Rocher

1250 avenue de Docteur Mathevet, F-85560 Longeville-sur-Mer (Vendée)
t: 02 51 90 31 57   e: **info@campinglepetitrocher.com**
alanrogers.com/FR85000   www.campinglepetitrocher.com

Accommodation: ☑Pitch ☑Mobile home/chalet ☐ Hotel/B&B ☐ Apartment

A former municipal site, Le Petit Rocher is now under the same management
(M. Guignard) as another local campsite, Les Brunelles. With its seaside location set in
a pine forest, there is an air of peace and tranquillity. Although the area is undulating, the
150 good size touring pitches are flat and arranged on terraces throughout the wooded
area. Electricity hook-ups are available (Euro style plugs) and there are adequate water
points. A grassy play area for children is thoughtfully situated in a hollow, but has
limited equipment. A fun pool was added in 2008. There are 28 unusual bungalows
for rent which would not be out of place on a safari. Square in shape and of wooden
construction they consist of a kitchen/living area and two bedrooms. Although some
do not have sanitary facilities, there are ample facilities on the site.

You might like to know

Near to Plage du Rocher, one of three safe
family beaches in this area backed by pine
forests with cycle tracks and also ideal for
hiking and horse riding.

☐ Beach on site
☑ Beach within 1 km.

☑ Sandy beach
☐ Blue Flag quality
☑ **Lifeguard** *(high season)*
☐ Sun lounger/deckchair hire
☑ Watersports
   (e.g. sailing, windsurfing)
☑ Snacks and drinks
☐ Sunshades
☑ **Dogs allowed** *(on the beach)*

Facilities: Three new, spacious sanitary blocks
are clean and well maintained with showers,
British style WCs. Facilities for people with
disabilities. Washing machine and dryer. Bar,
restaurant and takeaway (July/Aug). Tennis
court. New heated outdoor pool (8/5-11/9).
Max. 1 dog. Off site: Beach 200 m. Bars,
restaurant, and small shops nearby. Riding
and bicycle hire 2 km. Boat launching 11 km.
Fishing 15 km. Golf 20 km.

Open: 8 May - 11 September.

Directions: From Longeville-sur-Mer follow signs
for Le Rocher towards La Tranche-sur-Mer. Turn
right at first roundabout, following campsite signs
to site on right. GPS: 46.403767, -1.507183

Charges guide

Per unit incl. 2 persons and electricity	€ 16,00 - € 24,00
extra person	€ 3,00 - € 5,00
child (0-4 yrs)	free - € 3,00
dog	€ 3,00

Camping du Jard

123 Boulevard Maréchal de Lattre de Tassigny, F-85360 La Tranche-sur-Mer (Vendée)
t: **02 51 27 43 79** e: **info@campingdujard.fr**
alanrogers.com/FR85020 www.campingdujard.fr

Accommodation: ☑Pitch ☑Mobile home/chalet ☐ Hotel/B&B ☐ Apartment

Camping du Jard is a well maintained site between La Rochelle and Les Sables d'Olonne. First impressions are good, with a friendly welcome from M. Marton or his staff. The 160 touring pitches, all with electricity and 60 also with water and drainage, are level and grassy; many are hedged by bushes and a large variety of trees provide shade in places. An impressive pool complex has a heated outdoor pool with toboggan and paddling pool, plus an indoor pool with jacuzzi. The site is 700 m. from a sandy beach, with many shops and restaurants nearby. A short drive away is the fashionable resort of Les Sables d'Olonne, with its fine sandy beach, its good quality shops and restaurants and its visitor attractions. In fact, the entire Vendée region provides a wide range of well-documented activities and tourist destinations. Prime among these is the historical theme park Le Puy du Fou. In complete contrast, a wonderful day out can be had on the peaceful, shady waterways of the Marais Poitevin (La Venise Verte).

You might like to know
The site is near 13 km. of sandy beach which face toward the Ile de Ré. There are 700 m. of cycle paths from the sea shore to the Marais Poitevin.

☐ Beach on site
☑ Beach within 1 km.
☑ Sandy beach
☑ Blue Flag quality
☑ Lifeguard *(high season)*
☐ Sun lounger/deckchair hire
☑ Watersports
  (e.g. sailing, windsurfing)
☑ Snacks and drinks
☐ Sunshades
☐ Dogs allowed *(on the beach)*

Facilities: Three toilet blocks (only one open in low season) provide basic facilities for babies and disabled visitors. Laundry facilities. Motorhome service point. Shop (1/6-10/9), restaurant and bar (25/5-10/9). Heated outdoor pool (from 25/5); heated indoor pool (all season) . Sauna, solarium and fitness room. Tennis. Minigolf. Bicycle hire. Play area, games and TV rooms. Internet point; free WiFi around bar. American motorhomes not accepted. No pets.
Off site: Beach 700 m. Fishing and boat launching 1 km. Sailing 3 km. Riding 10 km. Golf 20 km.

Open: 26 April - 15 September.

Directions: La Tranche-sur-Mer is 40 km. southeast of Les Sables d'Olonne. From the A87 Cholet/La Roche-sur-Yon leave at exit 32 for La Tranche sur Mer and take D747 to La Tranche. Turn east following signs for La Faute-sur-Mer along bypass. Take exit for La Grière and then turn east to site.
GPS: 46.34836, -1.38738

Charges guide

Per unit incl. 2 persons, water and electricity	€ 25,50 - € 34,90
extra person	€ 4,50 - € 5,50
child (under 5 yrs)	€ 3,00 - € 4,00

Camping la Forêt

190 chemin de la Rive, F-85160 Saint Jean-de-Monts (Vendée)
t: 02 51 58 84 63 e: camping-la-foret@wanadoo.fr
alanrogers.com/FR85360 www.hpa-laforet.com

Accommodation: ☑Pitch ☑Mobile home/chalet ☐Hotel/B&B ☐ Apartment

Camping La Forêt is an attractive, well run site with a friendly family atmosphere, thanks to the hard working owners M. and Mme. Jolivet. It provides just 63 pitches with 39 for touring units. They are of a reasonable size and surrounded by mature hedges; all have water and electricity, and some also have drainage. A variety of trees provides shade to every pitch. There are 13 mobile homes for rent. The site has a quiet and relaxed atmosphere. La Forêt is an ideal choice for couples or families with young children wanting to be close to the sea but not looking for on-site entertainment and activities. The owners run their site on sound ecological principles and have invested heavily in measures to save energy and help the environment. The beach is just a 400 m. walk away, while the lively resort of Saint Jean-de-Monts with a wide choice of shops, bars and restaurants plus daily markets is just 6 km. away. Possible days out include a boat trip to the Ile d'Yeu or a gentle drive up the coast to the attractive Ile de Noirmoutier (reached by bridge or, at low tide, a causeway).

You might like to know

Fine sandy beach, away from the public gaze and frequented by nature lovers. Great sporting events on Grande Plage at Saint Jean-de-Monts: triathlon, sand sculpture, beach volleyball, sand yachting, riding etc.

- ☐ Beach on site
- ☑ Beach within 1 km.
- ☑ Sandy beach
- ☑ Blue Flag quality
- ☐ Lifeguard (high season)
- ☐ Sun lounger/deckchair hire
- ☑ Watersports (e.g. sailing, windsurfing)
- ☑ Snacks and drinks
- ☑ Sunshades
- ☑ Dogs allowed (on the beach)

Facilities: The central toilet block includes hot showers and washbasins in cubicles. Laundry and dishwashing facilities. Baby bath. Facilities for disabled visitors. Motorcaravan waste tanks can be emptied on request. Basic provisions sold in reception, including fresh bread. Takeaway (15/5-15/9). Small heated swimming pool (15/5-15/9). Small games room with TV. WiFi throughout from 2011 (charged). Play area. Bicycle hire. Only gas and electric barbecues allowed. Not suitable for American motorhomes. Off site: Beach 400 m. Network of cycle paths through the forest and local marshland. Sailing 1 km. Golf 2 km. Riding 3 km.

Open: 1 May - 28 September.

Directions: The site is 6 km. north of St Jean just off the D38 towards Notre Dame-de-Monts. At southern end of Notre Dame, turn west at sign for site and Plage de Pont d'Yeu. Bear left and site is on left in about 200 m.
GPS: 46.80807, -2.11384

Charges guide

Per unit incl. 2 persons and electricity	€ 21,90 - € 31,90
extra person	€ 3,50 - € 5,00
child (under 7 yrs)	€ 3,50 - € 3,90
dog	€ 2,50

Camping les Brunelles

Le Bouil, F-85560 Longeville-sur-Mer (Vendée)
t: 02 51 33 50 75 e: camping@les-brunelles.com
alanrogers.com/FR85440 www.camp-atlantique.com

Accommodation: ☑Pitch ☑Mobile home/chalet ☐Hotel/B&B ☐Apartment

This is a well managed site with good facilities and a varied programme of high season entertainment for all the family. A busy site in high season, there are plenty of activities to keep children happy and occupied. In 2007 Les Brunelles was combined with an adjacent campsite to provide 600 pitches of which 200 are for touring units; all have electricity (10A) and 20 of the new touring pitches also have water and waste. All are in excess of 100 m² to allow easier access for larger units. On the original Les Brunelles site, the touring pitches are all level on sandy grass and separated by hedges, away from most of the mobile homes. A large aquapark provides a swimming pool of 1,000 m² with slides, a sauna, steam room, jacuzzi, and a fitness centre. A good, supervised, sandy beach is 900 m. away.

You might like to know

There are three sandy beaches within easy reach, and also a number of surfing and sailing schools.

- ☐ Beach on site
- ☑ Beach within 1 km.
- ☑ Sandy beach
- ☐ Blue Flag quality
- ☐ Lifeguard *(high season)*
- ☐ Sun lounger/deckchair hire
- ☑ Watersports
  (e.g. sailing, windsurfing)
- ☐ Snacks and drinks
- ☐ Sunshades
- ☐ Dogs allowed *(on the beach)*

Facilities: Four old, but well maintained and modernised toilet blocks have British and Turkish style toilets and washbasins, both open style and in cabins. Laundry facilities. Shop, takeaway and large modern, airy bar (all season). Covered pool with jacuzzi (all season). Outdoor pool with slides and paddling pools (15/5-18/9). Tennis. Bicycle hire. Max. 1 dog. Off site: Riding 3 km. Golf 20 km. Good supervised sandy beach 900 m. St Vincent-sur-Jard 2 km.

Open: 3 April - 18 September.

Directions: From D21 (Talmont - Longueville), between St Vincent and Longueville, site signed south from main road towards coast. Turn left in Le Bouil (site signed). Site is 800 m. on left. GPS: 46.41330, -1.52313

Charges guide

Per unit incl. 2 persons and electricity	€ 21,00 - € 30,00
incl. water and drain	€ 25,00 - € 35,00
extra person	€ 5,00 - € 8,00
child (under 5 yrs)	free - € 5,00
animal	€ 5,00

Trevornick Holiday Park

Holywell Bay, Newquay TR8 5PW (Cornwall)
t: **01637 830531** e: **bookings@trevornick.co.uk**
alanrogers.com/UK0220 www.trevornick.co.uk

Accommodation: ☑Pitch ☐ Mobile home/chalet ☐ Hotel/B&B ☐ Apartment

Trevornick, once a working farm, is a modern, busy and well run family touring park providing a very wide range of amenities close to one of Cornwall's finest beaches. The park is well managed with facilities and standards constantly monitored. It has grown to provide caravanners and campers with 440 large grass pitches (350 with 10A electricity and 55 fully serviced) on five level fields and two terraced areas. There are no holiday caravans but 68 very well equipped 'Eurotents'. There are few trees, but some good views. Providing 'all singing, all dancing' facilities for fun packed family holidays, the farm buildings now provide the setting for the Farm Club. It provides much entertainment from bingo and quizzes to shows, discos and cabaret. The rest of the development provides a pool complex, an 18-hole golf course with a small, quiet club house offering bar meals and lovely views out to sea. An innovative idea is the 'Hire shop' where it is possible rent anything you might have forgotten from sheets, a fridge or travel cot to a camera or a wet suit to catch the famous Cornish surf!

You might like to know

Surfing is one of the most popular sports in Cornwall. Trevornick Holiday Park is only a short walk away from the beautiful Holywell Bay beach which attracts surfers from far and wide.

☐ **Beach on site**
☑ **Beach within 1 km.**

☑ **Sandy beach**
☐ **Blue Flag quality**
☐ **Lifeguard** (high season)
☐ **Sun lounger/deckchair hire**
☑ **Watersports**
    (e.g. sailing, windsurfing)
☑ **Snacks and drinks**
☐ **Sunshades**
☐ **Dogs allowed** (on the beach)

Facilities: Five modern toilet blocks provide showers (20p), two family bathrooms, baby bath, laundry facilities and provision for disabled visitors. Well stocked supermarket (from late May). Hire shop. Bars (with TV), restaurant, café and takeaway. Entertainment (every night in season). Pool complex with heated outdoor pool, paddling pool, sunbathing decks, solarium, sauna and massage chair. Health and beauty salon. Kiddies Club and indoor play area (supervised for 2-8 yr olds at a small charge). 18-hole pitch and putt with golf pro shop. Bicycle hire. Coarse fishing with three lakes. Only limited facilities open at Easter and from 8 Sept. Off site: Riding within 1 mile. Bicycle hire and boat launching 4 miles.

Open: Easter - mid September.

Directions: From A3075 approach to Newquay - Perranporth road, turn towards Cubert and Holywell Bay. Continue through Cubert to park on the right. GPS: 50.384983, -5.128933

Charges guide

Per person	£ 4,95 - £ 9,30
child (4-14 yrs)	£ 1,30 - £ 6,55
electricity	£ 4,75
'super' pitch incl. electricity	£ 8,95
dog	£ 3,45 - £ 3,75

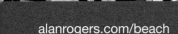

Woolacombe Sands Holiday Park

Beach Road, Woolacombe EX34 7AF (Devon)
t: 01271 870569 e: lifesabeach@woolacombe-sands.co.uk
alanrogers.com/UK0735 www.woolacombe-sands.co.uk

Accommodation: ☑Pitch ☑Mobile home/chalet ☐Hotel/B&B ☐Apartment

With sea views and within walking distance of Woolacombe's lovely sandy beach, this family park has been terraced out of the valley side as you drop down into the village. Apart from its smart entrance, it has been left natural. The pond and stream at the bottom are almost hidden with gated access to the National Trust fields across the valley. The 200 terraced level grass pitches all with 16A electricity are accessed by gravel roads with some good up and down walking needed to the toilet blocks (probably not the best environment for disabled visitors). Some 50 mobile homes and 14 bungalows are in the more central area, and tents tend to be placed on the bottom terraces. The park boasts both indoor and outdoor pools (accessed by code) with a full time attendant. Evenings see Woolly Bear emerge from his 'shack' to entertain children, with adult family entertainment later. A good plus factor is the fact that all facilities open when the site opens. A useful path leads from the site to the beach via the car park and the walk is said to take 15 minutes.

You might like to know

Situated on the North Devon coast two miles west of Bideford, The BIG Sheep is a leading member of Devon's Top Attractions and known as one of the best for families.

☐ Beach on site
☑ Beach within 1 km.
☑ Sandy beach
☑ Blue Flag quality
☑ Lifeguard *(high season)*
☐ Sun lounger/deckchair hire
☑ Watersports
  (e.g. sailing, windsurfing)
☑ Snacks and drinks
☐ Sunshades
☑ Dogs allowed *(on the beach)*

Facilities: Four basic toilet blocks with good hot water are spread amongst the terraces. The newer shower block has separate toilets opposite. Shop. Self-service food bar providing good value meals and breakfast (main season and B.Hs). Two bars and full entertainment programme. Heated indoor and outdoor pools both with paddling pool areas. Fenced play area on bark with plenty of equipment. Ball area with nets. Crazy golf. 'Kingpin' bowling. Off site: Beach 15 minutes walk or 0.5 miles. Riding next door. Golf, bicycle hire and freshwater fishing 0.5 miles.

Open: 1 April - 30 October.

Directions: Follow the A361 from Barnstaple through Braunton towards Ilfracombe. At Mullacott Cross roundabout turn left for Woolacombe (B3343). Site clearly signed on left as you go down the hill into the village. GPS: 51.17145, -4.191833

Charges guide

Per person (incl. electricity)	£ 5,00 - £ 15,00
child (4-15 yrs)	£ 2,50 - £ 7,50
dog	£ 5,00

Beverley Park

Goodrington Road, Paignton TQ4 7JE (Devon)
t: **01803 661978** e: **info@beverley-holidays.co.uk**
alanrogers.com/uk0870 www.beverley-holidays.co.uk

Accommodation: ☑ Pitch ☑ Mobile home/chalet ☐ Hotel/B&B ☐ Apartment

Beverley Park is an amazing holiday centre catering for every need. It is popular, busy and attractively landscaped with marvellous views over Torbay. The pools, a large dance hall, bars and entertainment, are all run in an efficient and orderly manner. The park has 187 caravan holiday homes and 23 lodges, mainly around the central complex. There are 172 touring pitches in the lower areas of the park, all reasonably sheltered, some with views across the bay and some on slightly sloping ground. All pitches can take awnings and 87 have 16A electricity (15 m. cable), 38 have hardstanding and 42 are fully serviced. Entertainment is organised at Easter and from early May. There are indoor and outdoor pools, each one heated and supervised. The Oasis fitness centre provides a steam room, jacuzzi, sun-bed and an excellent fitness room. The park is in the heart of residential Torbay, with views across the bay to Brixham and Torquay, and sandy beaches less than a mile away. This popular park has lots to offer and is well maintained and run. A member of the Best of British group.

You might like to know

No visit to Devon would be complete without a day at Dartmoor's famous Becky Falls, where there really is something for everyone to enjoy. Set within a spectacular ancient valley, the Falls have been attracting visitors for over 100 years.

☐ Beach on site

☑ Beach within 1 km.

☑ Sandy beach

☑ Blue Flag quality

☐ Lifeguard *(high season)*

☐ Sun lounger/deckchair hire

☑ Watersports
(e.g. sailing, windsurfing)

☐ Snacks and drinks

☐ Sunshades

☐ Dogs allowed *(on the beach)*

Facilities: Good toilet blocks adjacent to the pitches, well maintained and heated, include roomy showers, some with washbasins en-suite. Baths on payment. Unit for disabled visitors. Facilities for babies. Laundry. Gas supplies. Motorcaravan service point. Large general shop (29/3-29/10). Restaurant, bars and takeaway (all Easter, then 30/4-29/10, and Autumn half-term). Heated swimming pools (outdoor 28/5-4/9, indoor all year). Fitness centre. Tennis. Crazy golf. Playground. Nature trail. Amusement centre. Soft play area. Dogs are not accepted. Off site: Fishing, bicycle hire, riding and golf all within 2 miles.

Open: All year.

Directions: Park is south of Paignton in Goodrington Road between A379 coast road and B3203 ring road and is well signed on both. GPS: 50.413533, -3.568667

Charges guide

Per unit incl. 2 persons and electricity	£ 15,10 - £ 32,30
tent pitch incl. 2 persons	£ 12,60 - £ 28,20
extra person	£ 4,70
child	£ 3,50

Max. 6 persons per reservation.

Northam Farm Touring Park

Brean Sands, TA8 2SE Burnham-on-Sea (Somerset)
t: 01278 751244 e: enquiries@northamfarm.co.uk
alanrogers.com/UK1570 www.northamfarm.co.uk

Accommodation: ☑Pitch ☑Mobile home/chalet ☐Hotel/B&B ☐Apartment

Brean has been a popular holiday destination for decades and many large campsites have evolved. Northam Farm, owned by the Scott family, is one of them. It is a large family park with good facilities and an ongoing programme of improvements. Of the 750 pitches, 300 are for seasonal units and these are separated from the four touring fields. Pitches are well established and many have block paved hardstanding. There are two play areas for youngsters, a playing field, bicycle track and football pitch for teenagers, and fishing on the lake for adults. The owners and staff are always available to help visitors enjoy their stay. A monthly newsletter is published giving details of 'what's on' both on and off site. About 500 yards down the road is The Seagull, which is also owned by Northam Farm. Here you'll find an excellent restaurant, bar and nightly live entertainment, even during the low season. Just down the road is Brean Leisure Park with its swimming complex, funfair, golf and much more.

You might like to know

Ideally situated to discover Somerset, a county of real diversity. Unmissable attractions include Cheddar Caves and Gorge, Wookey Hole, Wells Cathedral, Glastonbury Tor plus traditional cider farms, museums and castles.

☐ **Beach on site**

☑ **Beach within 1 km.**

☑ **Sandy beach**

☐ **Blue Flag quality**

☐ **Lifeguard** (high season)

☐ **Sun lounger/deckchair hire**

☐ **Watersports**
 (e.g. sailing, windsurfing)

☐ **Snacks and drinks**

☐ **Sunshades**

☑ **Dogs allowed** (on the beach)

Facilities: Three good toilet blocks, well maintained and within reasonable distance of all pitches, provide ample toilets, washbasins and spacious showers (50p). Bathrooms (£1 charge). Baby room. Rooms for visitors with disabilities (radar key access). Laundry. Motorcaravan service point. Dog shower and two exercise areas. Licensed shop well stocked with food, holiday gear and accessories. Snack bar/takeaway. Free entry to live entertainment at The Seagull. Games room. Two play areas. Playing field. Fishing lake. A bus stops at the entrance. Off site: Beach 200 m. across road. Burnham-on-Sea 4 miles. Weston-super-Mare 8 miles. Golf, bicycle hire and riding 0.5 miles.

Open: March - October.

Directions: From M5 junction 22 follow signs to Burnham-on-Sea, Berrow and then Brean. Continue through Brean and Northam Farm is on the right, half a mile past Brean Leisure Park. GPS: 51.2949, -3.010167

Charges guide

Per unit incl. 2 persons and electricity	£ 7,75 - £ 24,00
extra person	£ 2,00 - £ 2,50
child (0-15 yrs)	£ 1,00

Lytton Lawn Touring Park

Lymore Lane, Milford-on-Sea SO41 0TX (Hampshire)
t: **01590 648331** e: **holidays@shorefield.co.uk**
alanrogers.com/UK2280 www.shorefield.co.uk

Accommodation: ☑Pitch ☑Mobile home/chalet ☐Hotel/B&B ☐Apartment

Lytton Lawn is the touring arm of Shorefield Country Park, a nearby holiday home park and leisure centre. Set in eight acres, it provides 135 marked pitches. These include 53 'premier' pitches (hardstanding, 16A electricity, pitch light, water and waste water outlet) in a grassy, hedged area – this section with its heated toilet block is open for a longer season. The rest of the pitches, all with electricity, are in the adjoining, but separate, gently sloping field, edged with mature trees and hedges and with a further toilet block. The larger reception and well stocked shop make this a good, comfortable, self sufficient site. Visitors to Lytton Lawn are entitled to use the comprehensive leisure facilities at Shorefield itself (2.5 miles away). These include a very attractive indoor pool, solarium, sauna and spa, fitness classes and treatments, all weather tennis courts, outdoor pools, restaurant facilities including a bistro (Easter-November), and entertainment and activity programmes. These are of a very good standard and mostly free (extra charges are made for certain activities).

Special offers
Free use of facilities at our main park 2.5 miles away. Please see website for special offers.

You might like to know
Bournemouth beach is 12 miles away. The New Forest is just 2 miles inland.

☐ Beach on site
☐ Beach within 1 km.

☐ Sandy beach
☐ Blue Flag quality
☐ Lifeguard *(high season)*
☐ Sun lounger/deckchair hire
☑ **Watersports**
  (e.g. sailing, windsurfing)
☐ Snacks and drinks
☐ Sunshades
☑ **Dogs allowed** *(on the beach)*

Facilities: Two modern toilet blocks are well fitted. Washing machine and dryer. Baby changing. Facilities for disabled visitors (Radar key). Motorcaravan service point. Shop (all year). Small fenced play area and hedged field with goal posts. Euro tents for rent. Only one dog per pitch is accepted. Off site: Village pub 10 minutes walk. Golf, riding, coarse fishing (all within 3 miles), sailing, windsurfing and boat launching facilities (1.5 miles). The New Forest, Isle of Wight, Bournemouth, Southampton are nearby. The beach at Milford-on-Sea is 1.7 miles.

Open: All year excl. 2 January - 6 Feburary.

Directions: From M27 follow signs for Lyndhurst and Lymington on A337. Continue towards New Milton and Lytton Lawn is signed at Everton; Shorefield is signed at Downton. GPS: 50.73497, -1.61803

Charges guide

Per unit incl. all persons and electricity,	£ 11,00 - £ 34,00
premier pitch incl. water, drainage and TV connection	£ 13,50 - £ 37,50
dog (max. 1)	£ 1,50 - £ 3,00

Less 40% Mon - Thurs in certain periods.
Min. weekly charge at busy times.

UNITED KINGDOM – Cromer

Woodhill Park

Cromer Road, East Runton, Cromer NR27 9PX (Norfolk)
t: 01263 512242 e: info@woodhill-park.com
alanrogers.comUK3500 www.woodhill-park.com

Accommodation: ☑Pitch ☑Mobile home/chalet ☐Hotel/B&B ☐Apartment

Woodhill is a seaside site with good views and a traditional atmosphere. It is situated on the cliff top, in a large, gently sloping, open grassy field, with 300 marked touring pitches. Of these, 210 have electricity (16A), seven are fully serviced and many have wonderful views over the surrounding countryside. A small number of holiday homes which are located nearer to the cliff edge have the best sea views, although perhaps at times a little bracing! Although the site is fenced there is access to the cliff top path (watch young children). It is possible locally to take a boat trip to see the seals off Blakeney Point. Nearby attractions include the Shire Horse Centre at West Runton and the North Norfolk Steam Railway.

You might like to know
The site overlooks a long sandy beach with rock pools – ideal for crabbing. There are many coastal walks to enjoy and nearby there are trips to see the seals at Blakeney Point.

- ☐ Beach on site
- ☑ Beach within 1 km.
- ☑ Sandy beach
- ☐ Blue Flag quality
- ☑ Lifeguard *(high season)*
- ☐ Sun lounger/deckchair hire
- ☑ Watersports
  (e.g. sailing, windsurfing)
- ☑ Snacks and drinks
- ☐ Sunshades
- ☐ Dogs allowed *(on the beach)*

Facilities: The three sanitary units are fully equipped but could be a little short of showers at peak times. Laundry with washing machines and dryer (iron from reception). Fully equipped unit for disabled persons. Well stocked shop (19/3-31/8). Good, large adventure playground and plenty of space for ball games. Crazy golf. Giant chess and golf course adjacent to the site.
Off site: Beach 0.5 miles. Fishing 1 mile. Bicycle hire, golf and riding 2 miles.

Open: 19 March - 31 October.

Directions: Site is beside the A149 coast road between East and West Runton.
GPS: 52.93307, 1.27664

Charges guide

Per unit incl. 2 persons and electricity	£ 14,80 - £ 17,65
extra person	£ 2,50
child (4-16 yrs)	£ 1,00
dog	£ 2,00 - £ 3,50

Hendre Mynach Touring Park

Llanaber, Barmouth LL42 1YR (Gwynedd)
t: **01341 280262** e: **mynach@lineone.net**
alanrogers.com/UK6370 www.hendremynach.co.uk

Accommodation: ☑Pitch ☑Mobile home/chalet ☐Hotel/B&B ☐Apartment

A neat and tidy family park, colourful flowers and top rate facilities make an instant impression on arrival down the steep entrance to this park (help is available to get out if you are worried). The 240 pitches are allocated in various areas, with substantial tenting areas identified. 40 gravel hardstandings are available and around the park there are 110 electricity hook-ups (10A), 20 fully serviced pitches and ample water taps. The beach is only 100 yards away but a railway line runs between this and the park. It can be crossed by pedestrian operated gates which could be a worry for those with young children. The quaint old seaside and fishing town of Barmouth is about a 30 minute walk along the prom. Here you will find 'everything'. Reception will provide leaflets with maps of local walks. Snowdonia National Park and mountain railway, the famous Ffestiniog railway, and castles and lakes everywhere provide plenty to see and do – this is a classic park in a classic area.

Facilities: Two toilet blocks, one modern and one traditional, both offer excellent facilities including spacious showers (free) and washbasins in cubicles. An extension to the traditional block has added a good unit for disabled visitors with ramp access. Motorcaravan service point. Well stocked shop incorporating a snack bar and takeaway (Easter-1/11). WiFi. Off site: Beach 100 m. Fishing, boat launching and bicycle hire within 0.5 miles. Riding 5 miles. Golf 9 miles.

Open: All year excl. 10 January - 28 February.

Directions: Park is off the A496 road north of Barmouth in village of Llanaber with entrance down a steep drive. GPS: 52.73300, -4.06618

Charges guide

Per unit incl. 2 persons and electricity	£ 16,00 - £ 29,00
extra person	£ 4,00
child (2-14 yrs)	£ 2,00
first dog free, extra dog	£ 1,00

Plus £2 per night for certain weekends.

You might like to know

Aberdovey was formerly an important shipbuilding town but is now a popular resort on the River Dyfi, with a fine blue flag beach.

☐ **Beach on site**
☑ **Beach within 1 km.**
☑ **Sandy beach**
☑ **Blue Flag quality**
☐ **Lifeguard** (high season)
☐ **Sun lounger/deckchair hire**
☑ **Watersports** (e.g. sailing, windsurfing)
☐ **Snacks and drinks**
☐ **Sunshades**
☐ **Dogs allowed** (on the beach)

Scourie Caravan & Camping Park

Harbour Road, Scourie IV27 4TG (Highland)
t: 01971 502060
alanrogers.com/UK7730

Accommodation: ☑Pitch ☐ Mobile home/chalet ☐ Hotel/B&B ☐ Apartment

Mr Mackenzie has carefully nurtured this park over many years, developing a number of firm terraces with 60 pitches which gives it an attractive layout – there is nothing regimented here. Perched on the edge of the bay in an elevated position, practically everyone has a view of the sea and a short walk along the shore footpath leads to a small sandy beach. The park has tarmac and gravel access roads, with well drained grass and hardstanding pitches, some with 10A electric hook-ups. A few are on an area which is unfenced from the rocks (young children would need to be supervised here). Mr Mackenzie claims that this is the only caravan park in the world from where, depending on the season, you can see palm trees, Highland cattle and Great Northern divers from your pitch. Red throated divers have also been seen. Trips to Handa Island (a special protection area for seabird colonies) are available from here and Tarbet. The clear water makes this area ideal for diving.

You might like to know

The small sandy beach is a short walk from the site. The water is crystal clear, great for swimming and fishing from the rocks. There is also a bird hide.

☐ Beach on site
☑ Beach within 1 km.

☑ Sandy beach
☐ Blue Flag quality
☐ Lifeguard (high season)
☐ Sun lounger/deckchair hire
☐ Watersports
  (e.g. sailing, windsurfing)
☐ Snacks and drinks
☐ Sunshades
☐ Dogs allowed (on the beach)

Facilities: The toilet facilities can be heated. Showers have no divider or seat. Laundry. Motorcaravan service point. The 'Anchorage' restaurant at the entrance to the park (used as reception at quiet times) serves meals at reasonable prices, cooked to order (I/4-30/9). Boat launching. Fishing permits can be arranged. Off site: Village with shop and post office, gas is available from the petrol station and mobile banks visit regularly.

Open: Easter/1 April - 30 September, but phone first to check.

Directions: Park is by Scourie village on the A894 road in northwest Sutherland. GPS: 58.351417, -5.156767

Charges guide

Per unit incl. 2 persons	£ 12,00 - £ 16,00
electricity	£ 2,00
extra person	£ 2,50
child (3-16 yrs)	£ 1,50

No credit cards.

IRELAND – Rosslare

St Margaret's Beach Caravan Park

Lady's Island, Rosslare Harbour (Co. Wexford)
t: 053 913 1169 e: info@campingstmargarets.ie
alanrogers.com/IR9170 www.campingstmargarets.ie

Accommodation: ☑Pitch ☑Mobile home/chalet ☐Hotel/B&B ☐Apartment

'This park is loved', was how a Swedish visitor described this environmentally-friendly, family-run caravan and camping park, the first the visitor meets near the Rosslare ferry port. Landscaping with flowering containers and maze-like sheltered camping areas and a pretty sanitary block all demonstrate the Traynor family's attention to detail. Most pitches give shelter from the fresh sea breeze and ferries can be seen crossing the Irish sea. Just metres away, the safe, sandy beach (part of the Wexford coastal path) curves around in a horseshoe shape ending in a small pier and slipway. Tourist information on the area is provided in the well stocked shop. The immediate area boasts of thatched roof cottages and cottage gardens. The park is an ideal base from which to explore the sunny southeast or as an overnight stop to prepare for touring Ireland or for departure. Local lakes and the Saltee Islands, various locations of ornithological interest, deep sea and shore fishing, and award-winning pubs and restaurants provide something for all.

You might like to know

The safe sandy beach is on the Wexford Coastal path. Lady's Island and lake, site of an ancient monastry, can be found around the coast. Also recommended are Kilmore Quay and Marina and Curracloe beach.

☐ **Beach on site**
☑ **Beach within 1 km.**
☑ **Sandy beach**
☐ **Blue Flag quality**
☐ **Lifeguard** (high season)
☐ **Sun lounger/deckchair hire**
☑ **Watersports**
   (e.g. sailing, windsurfing)
☐ **Snacks and drinks**
☐ **Sunshades**
☐ **Dogs allowed** (on the beach)

Facilities: The toilet block is spotless. Laundry room. Campers' kitchen including toaster, microwave and TV. Shop (June-Aug). Fresh milk and bread daily. Mobile homes for rent. Sun/TV room. Off site: Walking, beach and fishing. Boat slipway 2.5 km. Pitch and putt 2 km. Riding 6 km. Pubs and restaurants. The JFK Arboretum, Johnstown Castle and Gardens, the Irish National Heritage Park, Kilmore Quay and Marina, and Curracloe beach (featured in the film 'Saving Private Ryan').

Open: Mid March - 31 October.

Directions: From the N25 south of Wexford town, outside village of Tagoat, follow signs for Lady's Island and Carne. After 3 km. pass Butlers Bar and take next left and continue for 2.5 km. Site is well signed. GPS: 52.206433, -6.356417

Charges guide

Per unit incl. 2 persons and electricity	€ 20,00 - € 22,00
extra person	€ 2,50
child (2-16 yrs)	€ 1,50

Beara Camping The Peacock

Coornagillagh, Tuosist, Post Killarney (Co. Kerry)
t: 064 66842 87 e: bearacamping@eircom.net
alanrogers.com/IR9580 www.bearacamping.com

Accommodation: ☑Pitch ☑Mobile home/chalet ☐Hotel/B&B ☐Apartment

Five minutes from Kenmare Bay, The Peacock is a unique location for campers who appreciate the natural world, where disturbance to nature is kept to a minimum. This five-acre site offers simple, clean and imaginative camping facilities. Located on the Ring of Beara, bordering the counties of Cork and Kerry, visitors will be treated with hospitality by a Dutch couple, Bert and Klaske van Bavel, almost more Irish than the Irish, who have made Ireland their home and run the site with their family. The variety of accommodation at Beara Camping includes the hostel, caravan holiday homes, secluded hardstanding pitches with electricity and level grass areas for tenting. In addition, there are cabins sleeping two or four people and hiker huts sleeping two, ideal to avoid a damp night or to dry out. Bert and Klaske love to share with visitors the unspoiled natural terrain, its wildlife, the sheltered community campfire and advice on the walking and hiking routes in the area. Nearby are the Ring of Beara, stone circles, the Healy Pass, Ardea Castle, Derreen Gardens and the fishing town of Castletownbere.

Facilities: Three small blocks, plus facilities at the restaurant provide toilets, washbasins and free hot showers. Laundry service for a small fee. Campers' kitchens and sheltered eating area. Restaurant and takeaway (May-Oct). Pets are not permitted in rental accommodation or tents. Off site: Public transport from the gate during the summer months. Pub and shop 900 m. Riding 6 km. Golf 12 km. Boating, fishing and sea angling 200 m. Beach (pebble) 500 m.

Open: 1 April - 31 December.

Directions: From the A22, 17 km. east of Killarney, take the R569 south to Kenmare. In Kenmare take R571, Castletownbere road and site is 12 km. GPS: 51.8279, -9.7356

Charges guide

Per unit incl. 2 persons	
and electricity	€ 23,00
extra person	€ 3,50
child (0-10 yrs)	€ 2,00

You might like to know
This site is situated on the beautiful Beara Peninsula and only 5 km. from Kenmare Bay. Here you will find marine and wildlife including seals.

☐ Beach on site
☑ Beach within 1 km.
☐ Sandy beach
☐ Blue Flag quality
☐ Lifeguard *(high season)*
☐ Sun lounger/deckchair hire
☐ Watersports
   (e.g. sailing, windsurfing)
☐ Snacks and drinks
☐ Sunshades
☐ Dogs allowed *(on the beach)*

BELGIUM – Lombardsijde

Camping De Lombarde

Elisabethlaan 4, B-8434 Lombardsijde Middelkerke (West Flanders)
t: 058 236 839 e: info@delombarde.be
alanrogers.com/BE0560 www.delombarde.be

Accommodation: ☑Pitch ☑Mobile home/chalet ☐Hotel/B&B ☐Apartment

De Lombarde is a spacious, good value holiday site, between Lombardsijde and the coast. It has a pleasant atmosphere and modern buildings. The 380 pitches are set out in level, grassy bays surrounded by shrubs, all with electricity (16/20A), long leads may be needed. Vehicles are parked in separate car parks. There are many seasonal units and 21 holiday homes, leaving 180 touring pitches. There is a range of activities and an entertainment programme in season. This is a popular holiday area and the site becomes full at peak times. A pleasant stroll takes you into Lombardsijde. There is a tram service from near the site entrance to the town or the beach.

You might like to know
The site operates a tram service to the sandy beach and dunes which are 500 m. away.

☐ Beach on site
☑ Beach within 1 km.
☑ Sandy beach
☐ Blue Flag quality
☐ Lifeguard *(high season)*
☐ Sun lounger/deckchair hire
☑ Watersports
    (e.g. sailing, windsurfing)
☐ Snacks and drinks
☐ Sunshades
☐ Dogs allowed *(on the beach)*

Facilities: Three heated sanitary units are of an acceptable standard, with some washbasins in cubicles. Facilities for disabled people (but not for children). Large laundry. Motorcaravan services. Shop, restaurant/bar and takeaway (July/Aug. plus weekends and holidays 21/3-11/11). Tennis. Boules. Fishing lake. TV lounge. Animation programme for children. Playground. Internet access (in the bar). ATM. Torch useful. Only 1 dog accepted. Off site: Beach 400 m. Riding and golf 500 m. Bicycle hire 1 km.

Open: All year.

Directions: Coming from Westende, follow the tramlines. From traffic lights in Lombardsijde, turn left following tramlines into Zeelaan. Continue following tramlines until crossroads and tram stop, turn left into Elisabethlaan. Site is on right after 200 m. GPS: 51.15644, 2.75329

Charges guide

Per unit incl. 1-6 persons and electricity	€ 15,00 - € 28,50
dog (1 per pitch)	€ 2,60

BELGIUM – De Haan

Camping Ter Duinen

Wenduinsesteenweg 143, B-8421 De Haan (West Flanders)
t: 050 413 593   e: infolawrence.sansens@scarlet.com
alanrogers.com/BE0578   www.campingterduinen.be

Accommodation: ☑Pitch ☐ Mobile home/chalet ☐ Hotel/B&B ☐ Apartment

Camping Ter Duinen is a large, seaside holiday site with 120 touring pitches and over 700 privately owned static holiday caravans. The pitches are laid out in straight lines with tarmac access roads and the site has three immaculate toilet blocks. Other than a bar, and a playing field, the site has little else to offer, but it is only a 400 m. walk to the sea and next door to the site is a large sports complex with a sub-tropical pool and several sporting facilities. Opportunities for riding and golf (18-hole course) are close by. It is possible to hire bicycles in the town. The best places to visit for a day trip are Ostend with the Atlantic Wall from WWII, Knokke (where many summer festivals are held) and Bruges.

You might like to know
The campsite is ideally located for day trips to Bruges, Knokke and Ostend.

☐ Beach on site
☑ Beach within 1 km.

☑ Sandy beach

☐ Blue Flag quality

☐ Lifeguard *(high season)*

☐ Sun lounger/deckchair hire

☐ Watersports
  (e.g. sailing, windsurfing)

☐ Snacks and drinks

☐ Sunshades

☐ Dogs allowed *(on the beach)*

Facilities: Three modern toilet blocks have good fittings, washbasins in cubicles (hot and cold water) and showers (€ 1.20). Baby bath. Facilities for disabled visitors. Laundry facilities with two washing machines and a dryer, irons and ironing boards. Motorcaravan service point. Shop. Snack bar and takeaway. WiFi (charged). Off site: Sea with sandy beach 400 m. Bicycle hire 400 m. Riding 1 km. Golf 3 km. Boat launching 6 km. A bus for Bruges stops 200 m. from the site, a tram for the coast 400 m.

Open: 16 March - 15 October.

Directions: On E40 in either direction take exit for De Haan/Jabbeke. About 3 km. south of De Haan, turn at signs for campsites. GPS: 51.28318, 3.05753

Charges guide

Per unit incl. 2 persons and electricity	€ 17,00 - € 24,00
extra person	€ 2,50
child (under 10 yrs)	€ 2,00
dog	€ 3,00

NETHERLANDS – Katwijk

Camping Noordduinen

Campingweg 1, NL-2221 EW Katwijk (Zuid-Holland)
t: **0714 025 295** e: **info@noordduinen.nl**
alanrogers.com/NL5680 www.noordduinen.nl

Accommodation: ☑Pitch ☑Mobile home/chalet ☐Hotel/B&B ☐Apartment

This is a large, well managed site surrounded by dunes and sheltered partly by trees and shrubbery, which also separate the various camping areas. The 200 touring pitches are marked and numbered but not divided. All have electricity (10A) and 45 are fully serviced with electricity, water, drainage and TV connection. There are also seasonal pitches and mobile homes for rent. Entertainment is organised in high season for various age groups. A new complex with indoor and outdoor pools, a restaurant, small theatre and recreation hall provides a good addition to the site's facilities. Seasonal pitches and mobile homes are placed mostly away from the touring areas and are unobtrusive. You are escorted to an allocated pitch and sited in a formal layout and cars are parked away from the pitches. Bicycles can be hired nearby and worth a visit is Space Expo. The beaches are inviting and offer numerous possibilities for long walks and cycling tours.

You might like to know
The broad sandy beaches and sheltered dunes make this a beautiful area ideal for nature lovers and safe for young children.

☐ **Beach on site**
☑ **Beach within 1 km.**

☑ **Sandy beach**

☐ **Blue Flag quality**

☐ **Lifeguard** (high season)

☐ **Sun lounger/deckchair hire**

☐ **Watersports**
   (e.g. sailing, windsurfing)

☐ **Snacks and drinks**

☐ **Sunshades**

☐ **Dogs allowed** (on the beach)

Facilities: The three sanitary blocks are modern and clean, with washbasins in cabins, a baby room and provision for people with disabilities. Laundry. Motorcaravan services. Supermarket with fresh bread daily, bar, restaurant, takeaway (all 31/3-31/10). Recreation room. Swimming pool complex. Play area. Only gas barbecues are permitted. Dogs are not accepted.
Off site: Beach and fishing 300 m. Golf 6 km. Katwijk within walking distance. Riding 150 m.

Open: All year.

Directions: Leave A44 at exit 8 (Leiden - Katwijk) to join N206 to Katwijk. Take the Katwijk Noord exit and follow signs to site.
GPS: 52.21103, 4.40978

Charges guide

Per unit incl. 2 persons
and electricity   € 28,00 - € 36,00

Camping Tempelhof

Westerweg 2, NL-1759 JD Callantsoog (Noord-Holland)
t: 0224 581 522 e: info@tempelhof.nl
alanrogers.com/NL5735 www.tempelhof.nl

Accommodation: ☑Pitch ☑Mobile home/chalet ☐ Hotel/B&B ☐ Apartment

This first class site on the Dutch coast has 500 pitches with 250 for touring units, the remainder used by seasonal campers and a number of static units (mostly privately owned). All touring pitches have electricity (10/16A), water, drain and TV aerial point (40-90 m² but car free). Two pitches have private sanitary facilities. The grass pitches are arranged in long rows which are separated by hedges and shrubs, with access from hardcore roads. There is hardly any shade. There are facilities for many activities, including a heated indoor pool, a fitness room and tennis courts. Tempelhof is close to the North Sea beaches (1 km). In high season a full entertainment programme is arranged for children with water games, sports activities and music. With all these activities, you may not want to leave the site other than to go to the beach. However, the site is close to the ferry port of Den Helder where you can catch a ferry to the largest Dutch Island of Texel. Member of Leading Campings Group.

You might like to know

About one kilometre away is Callantsoog's sandy beach where, behind the dunes, you can sunbathe, play, swim, fly kites or go horse riding.

☐ Beach on site
☑ Beach within 1 km.
☑ Sandy beach
☐ Blue Flag quality
☐ Lifeguard *(high season)*
☐ Sun lounger/deckchair hire
☐ Watersports
  (e.g. sailing, windsurfing)
☐ Snacks and drinks
☐ Sunshades
☐ Dogs allowed *(on the beach)*

Facilities: Two modern toilet blocks include washbasins (open style and in cabins) and controllable hot showers (SEP key). Children's section and baby room. Private bathroom (€ 50 p/w). Facilities for disabled visitors. Fully equipped laundry. Motorcaravan services. Shop, restaurant, takeaway and bar (1/4-1/11). Swimming pool with paddling pool. Fitness room (€ 2,50). Recreation hall. Climbing wall. Tennis. Trim court. Play area. Extensive animation programme in high season. Internet access and WiFi. Bicycle hire. Max. 2 dogs. Off site: Fishing 500 m. Beach 1 km. Golf 6 km. Riding 4 km. Boat launching 1 km.

Open: All year.

Directions: From Alkmaar take the N9 road north towards Den Helder. Turn left towards Callantsoog on the N503 road and follow site signs. GPS: 52.846644, 4.715506

Charges guide

Per unit incl. 2 persons and electricity (plus meter)	€ 18,00 - € 36,00
extra person	€ 3,00
electricity per kWh	€ 0,35

Kennemer Duincamping De Lakens

Zeeweg 60, NL-2051 EC Bloemendaal aan Zee (Noord-Holland)
t: 0235 411 570 e: delakens@kennemerduincampings.nl
alanrogers.com/NL6870 www.kennemerduincampings.nl

Accommodation: ☑Pitch ☑Mobile home/chalet ☐Hotel/B&B ☐Apartment

De Lakens is part of de Kennemer Duincampings group and is beautifully located in the dunes at Bloemendaal aan Zee. This site has 940 reasonably large, flat pitches with a hardstanding of shells. There are 410 for tourers (235 with 16A electricity) and the sunny pitches are separated by low hedging. This site is a true oasis of peace in a part of the Netherlands usually bustling with activity. From this site it is possible to walk straight through the dunes to the North Sea. Although there is no pool, there is the sea. A separate area is provided for groups and youngsters to maintain the quiet atmosphere. It is not far to Amsterdam or Alkmaar and its cheese market. We feel you could have an enjoyable holiday here.

You might like to know

The beach of Bloemendaal aan Zee is popular for surfing. The Freestyle Frisbee World Championships have been held here.

☐ Beach on site
☑ Beach within 1 km.

☑ Sandy beach

☐ Blue Flag quality

☐ Lifeguard *(high season)*

☑ Sun lounger/deckchair hire

☐ Watersports
   (e.g. sailing, windsurfing)

☑ Snacks and drinks

☐ Sunshades

☐ Dogs allowed *(on the beach)*

Facilities: The six toilet blocks for touring units (two brand new) include controllable showers, washbasins (open style and in cabins), facilities for disabled people and a baby room. Launderette. Two motorcaravan service points. Bar/restaurant and snack bar. Supermarket. Adventure playgrounds. Bicycle hire. Entertainment program in high season for all. Dogs are not accepted. Off site: Beach and riding 1 km. Golf 10 km.

Open: 20 March - 1 November.

Directions: From Amsterdam go west to Haarlem and follow the N200 from Haarlem towards Bloemendaal aan Zee. Site is on the N200, on the right hand side.
GPS: 52.40563, 4.58652

Charges guide

Per unit incl. 4 persons	€ 14,10 - € 27,45
incl. electricity	€ 18,40 - € 28,70
extra person	€ 4,20

NETHERLANDS – Renesse

Camping International Renesse

Scharendijkseweg 8, NL-4325 LD Renesse (Zeeland)
t: 0111 461 391   e: info@camping-international.net
alanrogers.com/NL6950   www.camping-international.net

Accommodation: ☑Pitch ☑Mobile home/chalet ☐Hotel/B&B ☐Apartment

Situated 300 metres from the beach at Renesse in Zeeland, this is a friendly, family run site. Its owners have set high standards, which is demonstrated by the immaculate and tastefully decorated sanitary facilities. There are 200 pitches, all for touring units and with electricity connections (4-16A). These are a generous size and laid out in bays and avenues surrounded by hedging. Around a courtyard area beyond reception is a supermarket, and a bar which is attractively decorated with novel figures and the owner's personal memorabilia. Outside bench seating and umbrellas turns this corner of the site into a popular meeting place. Being close to one of Zeeland's excellent beaches makes this site an ideal choice for families.

You might like to know

The long sandy beaches and dunes are ideal for horse riding and even seal spotting – bring your binoculars!

☑ Beach on site

☐ Beach within 1 km.

☑ Sandy beach

☐ Blue Flag quality

☐ Lifeguard *(high season)*

☐ Sun lounger/deckchair hire

☑ Watersports
(e.g. sailing, windsurfing)

☐ Snacks and drinks

☐ Sunshades

☐ Dogs allowed *(on the beach)*

Facilities: Two luxury sanitary blocks provide showers, washbasins (some in cabins) and a baby room. Laundry room. Motorcaravan service point. Supermarket. Bar. Games room. TV. Play area. Bicycle hire. Entertainment in high season for all.

Open: 1 March - 31 October.

Directions: From Zierikzee follow N59 to Renesse for about 15 km. and turn right at roundabout (before town) onto local road signed R101. Continue for about 1 km. and turn left, then first right to site. GPS: 51.73981, 3.78912

Charges guide

Per unit incl. 2 persons	€ 26,40 - € 38,10
extra person	€ 4,75
child (2-9 yrs)	€ 4,00
electricity per kWh	€ 0,35
dog (max. 1)	€ 3,00

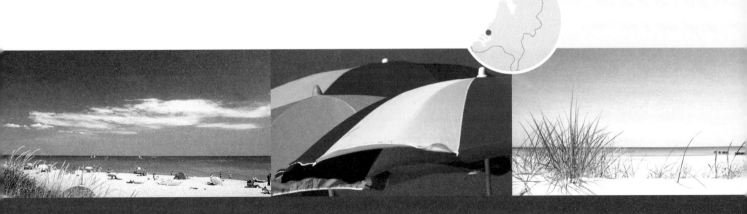

Camping De Krabbeplaat

Oude Veerdam 4, NL-3231 NC Brielle (Zuid-Holland)
t: **0181 412 363** e: **info@krabbeplaat.nl**
alanrogers.com/NL6980 www.krabbeplaat.nl

Accommodation: ☑Pitch ☑Mobile home/chalet ☐ Hotel/B&B ☐ Apartment

Camping de Krabbeplaat is a family run site situated near the ferry port in a wooded, recreation area next to the 'Brielse Meer' lake. There are 510 spacious pitches, with 100 for touring units, 68 with electricity (10A), cable connections and a water supply nearby. A separate field is used for groups of up to 450 guests. A nature conservation plan exists to ensure the site fits into its natural environment. The lake and its beaches provide the perfect spot for watersports and relaxation and the site has its own harbour where you can moor your own boat. The beach is 7 km. from the site for those who prefer the sea. Plenty of cultural opportunities can be found in the historic towns of the area. Because of the large range of amenities and the tranquil nature of the site, De Krabbeplaat is perfect for families and couples.

You might like to know

There is a small lake beach on site which is safe for children, however there are sea beaches 7 km. away.

☑ **Beach on site**
☐ **Beach within 1 km.**
☑ **Sandy beach**
☐ **Blue Flag quality**
☐ **Lifeguard** *(high season)*
☐ **Sun lounger/deckchair hire**
☑ **Watersports**
   (e.g. sailing, windsurfing)
☐ **Snacks and drinks**
☐ **Sunshades**
☐ **Dogs allowed** *(on the beach)*

Facilities: One large and two smaller heated toilet blocks in traditional style provide separate toilets, showers and washing cabins. High standards of cleanliness, a dedicated unit for disabled persons and provision for babies. Warm water is free of charge. Launderette. Motorcaravan services. Supermarket and snack bar (1/4-1/10). Restaurant (July/Aug). Recreation room. Youth centre. Tennis. Playground and play field. Animal farm. Bicycle and children's pedal hire. Canoe, surf, pedal boat and boat hire. Fishing. WiFi. Two cottages for hikers. No dogs are accepted.

Open: 27 March - 25 October.

Directions: From the Amsterdam direction take the A4 (Europoort), then the A15 (Europoort). Take exit for Brielle on N57 and, just before Brielle, site is signed. GPS: 51.9097, 4.18536

Charges 2011

Per unit incl. 2 persons and electricity	€ 17,00 - € 23,50
extra person	€ 3,20
child (under 12 yrs)	€ 2,70

Camping Wulfener Hals

Wulfener Hals Weg, D-23769 Wulfen auf Fehmarn (Schleswig-Holstein)
t: 043 718 6280 e: camping@wulfenerhals.de
alanrogers.com/DE3003 www.wulfenerhals.de

Accommodation: ☑ Pitch ☑ Mobile home/chalet ☐ Hotel/B&B ☐ Apartment

If you are travelling to Denmark or on to Sweden, taking the E47/A1 then B207 from Hamburg, and the ferry from Puttgarden to Rødbyhavn, this is a top class all year round site, either to rest overnight or as a base for a longer stay. Attractively situated by the sea, it is a large, mature site (34 hectares) and is well maintained. It has over 800 individual pitches of up to 160 m² (half for touring) in glades and some separated by bushes, with shade in the older parts, less in the newer areas nearer the sea. There are many hardstandings and 552 pitches have electricity, water and drainage. A separate area has been developed for motorcaravans. It provides 60 extra large pitches, all with electricity, water and drainage, and some with TV aerial points, together with a new toilet block. There is much to do for young and old alike at Wulfener Hals, with a new heated outdoor pool and paddling pool (unsupervised), although the sea is naturally popular as well. The site also has many sporting facilities including its own golf courses and schools for watersports. Member of Leading Campings Group.

You might like to know

Beach activities include sailing with catamarans, surfing and kite surfing, diving courses and wreck diving with professionals.

☑ Beach on site

☐ Beach within 1 km.

☑ Sandy beach

☐ Blue Flag quality

☑ Lifeguard *(high season)*

☐ Sun lounger/deckchair hire

☑ Watersports
  (e.g. sailing, windsurfing)

☑ Snacks and drinks

☐ Sunshades

☑ Dogs allowed *(on the beach)*

Facilities: Five heated sanitary buildings have first class facilities including showers and both open washbasins and private cabins. Family bathrooms for rent. Facilities for disabled visitors. Laundry. Motorcaravan services. Shop, bar, restaurants and takeaway (April-Oct). Swimming pool (May-Oct). Sauna. Solarium. Jacuzzi. Sailing, windsurfing and diving schools. Boat slipway. Golf courses (18 holes, par 72 and 9 holes, par 27). Riding. Fishing. Archery. Good play equipment for younger children. Bicycle hire. Catamaran hire. Off site: Naturist beach 500 m. Village minimarket 2 km.

Open: All year.

Directions: From Hamburg take A1/E47 north to Puttgarden, cross the bridge onto the island of Fehmarn and turn right twice to Avendorf and follow the signs for Wulfen and the site.
GPS: 54.40805, 11.17374

Charges guide

Per unit incl. 2 persons and electricity	€ 13,30 - € 44,40
extra person	€ 3,90 - € 8,40
child (2-13 yrs)	€ 2,30 - € 5,70
child (14-18 yrs)	€ 3,40 - € 7,30
dog	€ 1,00

Plus surcharges for larger pitches.

GERMANY – Fehmarn

Strandcamping Wallnau

Wallnau 1, D-23769 Fehmarn (Schleswig-Holstein)
t: 043 729 456 e: wallnau@strandcamping.de
alanrogers.com/DE3007 www.strandcamping.de

Accommodation: ☑Pitch ☑Mobile home/chalet ☐Hotel/B&B ☐Apartment

With direct beach access and protected from the wind by a dyke, this family site is on Germany's second largest island (since 1963 joined to the Baltic sea coast by a bridge). This is a quiet location on the western part of Fehmarn island in close proximity to a large bird sanctuary. Of the 800 pitches, 400 are for touring, all with electricity and on level grass areas arranged in alleys and separated by hedges. The island is low lying, ideal for leisurely walking or cycle riding, especially along the track that runs along the top of the dyke. The beach is a mixture of sand and pebbles and in summer lifeguards are on duty. The southern part is a naturist area. For those with an ornithological interest the bird sanctuary with over 80 species is worth visiting. Swimming, sailing and diving are possible in the sea and there is a windsurfing school. For those who prefer dry land there is pony riding for children and a riding school. In summer there are entertainment programmes for children and courses for adults, twice weekly film shows and a disco.

You might like to know
The site boasts a specialist kite and wind surfing school, its own dive centre and riding stables. The site is also located next to the bird sanctuary of Wallnau.

☑ **Beach on site**

☐ **Beach within 1 km.**

☐ **Sandy beach**

☐ **Blue Flag quality**

☑ **Lifeguard** *(high season)*

☐ **Sun lounger/deckchair hire**

☑ **Watersports**
  (e.g. sailing, windsurfing)

☐ **Snacks and drinks**

☐ **Sunshades**

☐ **Dogs allowed** *(on the beach)*

Facilities: Heated sanitary blocks (cleaning variable) provide free showers. Child size toilets and showers. Baby rooms. Facilities for disabled guests. Laundry facilities. Motorcaravan service points. Shop. Bar, restaurant and snack bar. Open air stage and soundproofed disco. Spa, solarium and sauna. Archery. Watersports. Minigolf. Internet café. WiFi. Beach fishing. Off site: Boat launching 6 km. Golf 15 km.

Open: 27 March - 25 October.

Directions: After crossing the bridge follow road to Landkirchen and Petersdorf. From Petersdorf site is signed. It is 4 km. northwest of the town. GPS: 54.48761, 11.0186

Charges guide

Per person	€ 4,00 - € 7,20
child (under 17 yrs)	€ 2,00 - € 6,30
pitch	€ 6,50 - € 17,00
electricity	€ 2,40
dog	€ 1,50 - € 5,00

No credit cards.

DENMARK – Blavand

Hvidbjerg Strand Camping

Hvidbjerg Strandvej 27, DK-6857 Blavand (Ribe)
t: 75 27 90 40   e: info@hvidbjerg.dk
alanrogers.com/DK2010   www.hvidbjerg.dk

Accommodation: ☑Pitch ☑Mobile home/chalet ☐Hotel/B&B ☐Apartment

A family owned, TopCamp holiday site, Hvidbjerg Strand is on the west coast near Blåvands Huk, 43 km. from Esbjerg. It is a high quality, seaside site with a wide range of amenities. Most of the 570 pitches have electricity (6/10A) and the 130 'comfort' pitches also have water, drainage and satellite TV. To the rear of the site, 70 new, fully serviced pitches have been developed, some up to 250 m² and 16 with private sanitary facilities. Most pitches are individual and divided by hedges in rows, on flat, sandy grass, with areas also divided by small trees and hedges. On-site leisure facilities include an indoor suite of supervised play rooms, designed for all ages with Lego, computers, video games, TV, etc. and an impressive, tropical style indoor pool complex. This includes stalactite caves and a 70 m. water chute (the 'Black Hole') with sounds and lights, plus water slides, spa baths, Turkish bath and a sauna. A Blue Flag beach and windsurfing school are adjacent to the site and the town offers a full activity programme during high season. Member of Leading Campings Group.

You might like to know
The special conditions here are due to the reef known as 'Horns Reef' stretching 40 kilometres into the North Sea and creating a lagoon on the south side.

☑ **Beach on site**

☐ **Beach within 1 km.**

☑ **Sandy beach**

☑ **Blue Flag quality**

☐ **Lifeguard** *(high season)*

☐ **Sun lounger/deckchair hire**

☐ **Watersports**
   (e.g. sailing, windsurfing)

☐ **Snacks and drinks**

☐ **Sunshades**

☐ **Dogs allowed** *(on the beach)*

Facilities: Five superb toilet units include washbasins (many in cubicles), roomy showers, spa baths, suites for disabled visitors, family bathrooms, kitchens and laundry facilities. The most recent units include a children's bathroom decorated with dinosaurs and Disney characters and racing car baby baths. Motorcaravan services. Supermarket. Café/restaurant. TV rooms. Pool complex, solarium and sauna. Play areas. Supervised play rooms (09.00-16.00 daily). Barbecue areas. Minigolf. Riding (Western style). Fishing. Dog showers. ATM machine. Off site: Legoland 70 km.

Open: 19 March - 24 October.

Directions: From Varde take roads 181/431 to Blåvand. Site is signed left on entering the town (mind speed bump on town boundary). GPS: 55.54600, 8.13507

Charges guide

Per unit incl. 2 persons and electricity	DKK 220,00 - 365,00
extra person	DKK 75,00
child (0-11 yrs)	DKK 55,00
dog	DKK 27,00

Klim Strand Camping

Havvejen 167, Klim Strand, DK-9690 Fjerritslev (Nordjylland)
t: 98 22 53 40 e: ksc@klim-strand.dk
alanrogers.com/DK2170 www.klim-strand.dk

Accommodation: ☑Pitch ☑Mobile home/chalet ☐Hotel/B&B ☐Apartment

A large family holiday site right beside the sea, Klim Strand is a paradise for children. It is a privately owned TopCamp site with a full complement of quality facilities, including its own fire engine and trained staff. The site has 460 numbered touring pitches, all with electricity (10A), laid out in rows, many divided by trees and hedges and shade in parts. Some 220 of these are fully serviced with electricity, water, drainage and TV hook-up. On site activities include an outdoor water slide complex, an indoor pool, tennis courts and pony riding (all free). A 'Wellness' spa centre is a recent addition. For children there are numerous play areas, an adventure playground with aerial cable ride and a roller skating area. There is a kayak school and a large bouncy castle for toddlers. Live music and dancing are organised twice a week in high season. Suggested excursions include trips to offshore islands, visits to local potteries, a brewery museum and bird watching on the Bygholm Vejle. Member of Leading Campings Group.

You might like to know
Bird reserve nearby and several inland lakes with boat trips available for fishing.

☑ **Beach on site**
☐ **Beach within 1 km.**

☑ **Sandy beach**
☑ **Blue Flag quality**
☐ **Lifeguard** (high season)
☐ **Sun lounger/deckchair hire**
☐ **Watersports**
   (e.g. sailing, windsurfing)
☐ **Snacks and drinks**
☐ **Sunshades**
☐ **Dogs allowed** (on the beach)

Facilities: Two good, large, heated toilet blocks are central, with spacious showers and some washbasins in cubicles. Separate children's room. Baby rooms. Bathrooms for families (some charged) and disabled visitors. Two smaller units are by reception and beach. Laundry. Well equipped kitchens and barbecue areas. TV lounges. Motorcaravan services. Pizzeria. Supermarket, restaurant and bar (all season). Pool complex. Sauna, solariums, whirlpool bath, hairdressing rooms, fitness room. Wellness centre. Internet cafe. TV rental. Play areas. Crèche. Bicycle hire. Cabins to rent. Off site: Golf 10 km. Boat launching 25 km.

Open: 26 March - 24 October.

Directions: Turn off the Thisted - Fjerritslev no. 11 road to Klim from where site is signed. GPS: 57.133333, 9.166667

Charges guide

Per unit incl. 2 persons and electricity	DKK 305 - 355
extra person	DKK 75
child (1-11 yrs)	DKK 55
dog	DKK 25

DENMARK – Fåborg

Bøjden Strand Ferie Park

Bøjden Landevej 12, Bøjden, DK-5600 Fåborg (Fyn)
t: 63 60 63 60   e: info@bojden.dk
alanrogers.com/DK2200   www.bojden.dk

Accommodation: ☑Pitch ☑Mobile home/chalet ☐Hotel/B&B ☐Apartment

Bøjden is located in one of the most beautiful corners of southwest Fyn (Funen in English), known as the 'Garden of Denmark'. This is a well equipped site separated from the beach only by a hedge. Bøjden is a delightful site for an entire holiday, while remaining a very good centre for excursions. Arranged in rows on mainly level grassy terraces and divided into groups by hedges and some trees, many pitches have sea views as the site slopes gently down from the road. The 295 pitches (210 for touring units) all have electricity (10A) and include 65 new, fully serviced pitches (water, drainage and TV aerial point). Four special motorcaravan pitches also have water and waste points. There are indoor and outdoor pools, the latter with a paddling pool and sun terrace open during suitable weather conditions. Everyone will enjoy the beach (Blue Flag) for swimming, boating and watersports. The water is too shallow for shore fishing but boat trips can be arranged.

You might like to know
The campsite has its own kayak school, a modern indoor and outdoor pool complex and is convenient for day trips to Fåborg, which is a wonderful old seaport.

☑ **Beach on site**

☐ **Beach within 1 km.**

☐ **Sandy beach**

☑ **Blue Flag quality**

☐ **Lifeguard** (high season)

☐ **Sun lounger/deckchair hire**

☑ **Watersports**
(e.g. sailing, windsurfing)

☐ **Snacks and drinks**

☐ **Sunshades**

☐ **Dogs allowed** (on the beach)

Facilities: The superb quality, central toilet block includes washbasins in cubicles, controllable showers, family bathrooms (some with whirlpools and double showers), baby room and excellent facilities for disabled people. Well appointed kitchen and laundry. A new unit serves a recent extension to the site. An older unit near reception provides extra facilities and a further kitchen. Motorcaravan services. Supermarket. Licensed restaurant. Takeaway. Indoor and outdoor swimming pools. Solarium. Well equipped, fenced toddler play area and separate adventure playground. TV and games rooms. Internet café and WiFi. Barbecue area. Fishing. Minigolf. Off site: Beach adjacent. Bicycle hire and riding 10 km. Golf 12 km.

Open: 14 March - 20 October.

Directions: From Fåborg follow road no. 8 to Bøjden and site is on right 500 m. before ferry terminal (from Fynshav).
GPS: 55.105289, 10.107808

Charges guide

Per person	DKK 67
child (0-11 yrs)	DKK 45
pitch	DKK 10 - 100
electricity	DKK 31

Credit cards accepted with 5% surcharge.

TopCamp Feddet

Feddet 12, DK-4640 Faxe (Sjælland)
t: 56 72 52 06 e: info@feddetcamping.dk
alanrogers.com/DK2255 www.feddetcamping.dk

Accommodation: ☑Pitch ☑Mobile home/chalet ☐ Hotel/B&B ☐ Apartment

This interesting, spacious site with ecological principles is located on the Baltic coast. It has a fine, white, sandy beach (Blue Flag) which runs the full length of one side, with the Præstø fjord on the opposite side of the peninsula. There are 413 pitches for touring units, generally on sandy grass, with mature pine trees giving adequate shade. All have 10A electricity and 20 are fully serviced (water, electricity, drainage and sewage). Two recently constructed sanitary buildings which have been specially designed, are clad with larch panels from sustainable local trees and are insulated with flax mats. They have natural ventilation, with ventilators controlled by sensors for heat, humidity and smell. All this saves power and provides a comfortable climate inside. Heating, by a wood chip furnace (backed up by a rape seed oil furnace), is CO_2 neutral and replaces 40,000 litres of heating oil annually. Taps are turned off automatically, lighting is by low wattage bulbs with PIR switching. Recycling is also very important here.

You might like to know
For a complete change, why not try abseiling?

- ☑ Beach on site
- ☐ Beach within 1 km.
- ☑ Sandy beach
- ☑ Blue Flag quality
- ☐ Lifeguard *(high season)*
- ☐ Sun lounger/deckchair hire
- ☐ Watersports
  (e.g. sailing, windsurfing)
- ☐ Snacks and drinks
- ☐ Sunshades
- ☐ Dogs allowed *(on the beach)*

Facilities: Both sanitary buildings are impressive, equipped to a very high standard. Family bathrooms (with twin showers), complete suites for small children and babies. Facilities for disabled campers. Laundry. Kitchens, dining room and TV lounge. Excellent motorcaravan service point. Well stocked licensed shop. Licensed bistro and takeaway (1/5-20/10 but weekends only outside peak season). Minigolf. Games room. Indoor playroom and several playgrounds for all ages. Event camp for children. Pet zoo. WiFi. Massage. Watersports. Fishing. Off site: Abseiling, pool. Amusement park.

Open: All year.

Directions: From the south on the E47/55 take exit 38 towards Præstø. Turn north on 209 road towards Fakse and from Vindbyholt follow site signs. From the north on the E47/55 take exit 37 east towards Fakse. Just before Fakse turn south on 209 road and from Vindbyholt, site signs. GPS: 55.17497, 12.10203

Charges guide

Per unit incl. 2 persons and electricity	DKK 250 - 323
extra person	DKK 72
child (0-11 yrs)	DKK 50 - 105
dog	DKK 20

First Camp Båstad-Torekov

Flymossa Vagen 5, S-260 93 Torekov (Skåne Län)
t: 043 136 4525   e: torekov@firstcamp.se
alanrogers.com/SW2640   www.firstcamp.se

Accommodation: ☑Pitch ☑Mobile home/chalet ☐Hotel/B&B ☐Apartment

Part of the First Camp chain, this site is 500 m. from the fishing village of Torekov, 14 km. west of the home of the Swedish tennis WCT Open at Båstad, on the stretch of coastline between Malmö and Göteborg. Useful en route from the most southerly ports, it is a very good site and worthy of a longer stay for relaxation. It has 510 large pitches (390 for touring units), all numbered and marked, mainly in attractive natural woodland, with some on more open ground close to the shore. Of these, 300 have 10A electricity and cable TV, 77 also having water and drainage. The modern reception complex is professionally run and is also home for a good shop, a snack bar, restaurant, and pizzeria. The spacious site covers quite a large area and there is a cycle track along the shore to the bathing beach. Games for children are organised in high season and there is an outdoor stage for musical entertainment and dancing (also in high season). This well run site is a pleasant place to stay.

You might like to know

At nearby Torekov you can rent a fishing boat. Alternatively take a short boat ride to Halland Vadero for a seal safari or swim in the safe shallow water.

☑ **Beach on site**

☐ **Beach within 1 km.**

☑ **Sandy beach**

☐ **Blue Flag quality**

☐ **Lifeguard** (high season)

☐ **Sun lounger/deckchair hire**

☑ **Watersports**
   (e.g. sailing, windsurfing)

☐ **Snacks and drinks**

☐ **Sunshades**

☐ **Dogs allowed** (on the beach)

Facilities: Three very good sanitary blocks with facilities for babies and disabled visitors. Laundry. Cooking facilities and dishwashing. Motorcaravan service point. Bar. Restaurant, pizzeria and snack bar with takeaway (15/6-5/8). Shop and kiosk. Minigolf. Sports fields. Play areas and adventure park for children. Bicycle hire. TV room. Beach. Fishing. WiFi on all pitches. Off site: Tennis close. Golf 1 km. Riding 3 km. Games, music and entertainment in high season.

Open: 16 April - 26 September.

Directions: From the E6 Malmö - Göteborg road take the Torekov/Båstad exit and follow signs for 20 km. towards Torekov. Site is signed 1 km. before the village on the right.
GPS: 56.43097, 12.64055

Charges guide

Per unit incl. 4 persons	SEK 140 - 265
incl. electricity and TV connection	SEK 185 - 370

SWEDEN – Färjestaden

Krono Camping Saxnäs

S-386 95 Färjestaden (Kalmar Län)
t: 048 535 700 e: info@kcsaxnas.se
alanrogers.com/SW2680 www.kcsaxnas.se

Accommodation: ☑Pitch ☑Mobile home/chalet ☐Hotel/B&B ☐Apartment

Well placed for touring Sweden's Riviera and the fascinating and beautiful island of Öland, this family run site, part of the Krono group, has 420 marked and numbered touring pitches. Arranged in rows on open, well kept grassland dotted with a few trees, all have electricity (10/16A), 320 have TV connections and 112 also have water. An unmarked area without electricity can accommodate around 60 tents. The site has about 130 long stay units and cabins for rent. The sandy beach slopes very gently and is safe for children. Reception is efficient and friendly with good English spoken. In high season children's games are organised and dances are held twice weekly, with other activities on other evenings. Nearby attractions include the 7 km. long Öland road bridge and the 400 old windmills on the island (in the 19th century there were 2,000). The southern tip of Öland, Ottenby, is a paradise for bird watchers. Kalmar and its castle, museums and old town on the mainland, Eketorp prehistoric fortified village, Öland Djurpark, and the Swedish Royal family's summer residence, Solliden, are well worth a visit.

You might like to know
The gently sloping beach is safe for children and is cleaned on a daily basis. The Öland Animal and Amusement Park is 3 km. away.

☑ Beach on site

☐ Beach within 1 km.

☑ Sandy beach

☑ Blue Flag quality

☐ Lifeguard *(high season)*

☐ Sun lounger/deckchair hire

☐ Watersports
   (e.g. sailing, windsurfing)

☐ Snacks and drinks

☐ Sunshades

☐ Dogs allowed *(on the beach)*

Facilities: Three heated sanitary blocks provide a good supply of roomy shower cubicles, washbasins, some washbasin/WC suites and WCs. Facilities for babies and disabled visitors. Well-equipped laundry room. Good kitchen with cookers, microwaves and dishwasher (free), and sinks. Gas supplies. Motorcaravan services. Shop (1/5-30/8). Pizzeria, licensed restaurant and café (all 1/5-30/8). Bar (1/7-31/7). Swimming pool. Playgrounds. Bouncy castle. Boules. Fishing. Canoe hire. Bicycle hire. Minigolf. Family entertainment and activities. Off site: Golf 500 m. Riding 2 km.

Open: 16 April - 26 September.

Directions: Cross Öland road bridge from Kalmar on road no. 137. Take the exit for Öland Djurpark/Saxnäs, then follow campsite signs. The site is just north of the end of the bridge. GPS: 56.68727, 16.48182

Charges guide

Per unit incl. electricity	SEK 190 - 325

Weekend and weekly rates available.

Krono Camping Böda Sand

S-380 75 Byxelkrok (Kalmar Län)
t: 048 522 200   e: bodasand@kronocampingoland.se
alanrogers.com/SW2690   www.kronocampingoland.se

Accommodation: ☑Pitch ☑Mobile home/chalet ☐Hotel/B&B ☐Apartment

Krono Camping Böda Sand is beautifully situated at the northern end of the island of Øland and is one of Sweden's largest and most modern campsites. Most of the 1,300 pitches have electricity (10/16A) and TV connections, 130 have water and waste water drainage. The pitches and 123 cabins for rent are spread out in a pine forest, very close to the fabulous 10 km. long, white sand beach. Here you will also find a restaurant, kiosks, toilets and beach showers, and a relaxation centre with an indoor/outdoor pool. The reception, the toilet blocks and the services at this site are excellent and very comprehensive. Entertainment and activities both for children and adults are extensive – there are more than 90 different items to choose from every week during high season. For exercise, there are tennis and badminton courts, trim trails, a football pitch and a 9-hole golf course, par 58, in the forest. Nearby attractions are the lighthouse at the northern tip of Øland, the Troll forest and the lime stone natural sculptures at Byerum. Art galleries and craft shops are well worth a visit.

You might like to know

The white sandy beach is cleaned on a daily basis. The site offers diving lessons in the pool during high season.

☑ **Beach on site**

☐ **Beach within 1 km.**

☑ **Sandy beach**

☐ **Blue Flag quality**

☐ **Lifeguard** *(high season)*

☐ **Sun lounger/deckchair hire**

☑ **Watersports**
  (e.g. sailing, windsurfing)

☐ **Snacks and drinks**

☐ **Sunshades**

☐ **Dogs allowed** *(on the beach)*

Facilities: Seven heated sanitary blocks provide a good supply of roomy shower cubicles, washbasins, some washbasin suites and WCs. Facilities for babies and disabled visitors (key at reception). Well equipped laundry rooms. Excellent kitchens with cookers, ovens, microwaves, dishwashers (free) and sinks. Motorcaravan services. Supermarket and bakery. Pizzeria, café, pub and restaurant. Takeaway. Bicycle hire, pedal cars and pedal boat hire. WiFi. Minigolf. 9-hole golf course. Indoor/outdoor swimming pool (on the beach). Trim trails. Family entertainment and activities.

Open: 1 May - 1 October.

Directions: From Kalmar cross the Øland road bridge on road no. 137. On Øland follow road no. 136 towards Borgholm and Byxelkrok. Turn left at the roundabout north of Böda and follow the campsite signs to Krono camping Böda Sand. GPS: 57.27436, 17.04851

Charges guide

Per pitch	SEK 155 - 235
incl. electricity	SEK 195 - 285

FINLAND – Oulu

Nallikari Camping

PL55, FIN-90015 Oulu (Oulu)
t: 085 586 1350 e: nallikari.camping@ouka.fi
alanrogers.com/FI2970 www.nallikari.fi/FI/etusivu.html

Accommodation: ☑Pitch ☑Mobile home/chalet ☐ Hotel/B&B ☐ Apartment

This is probably one of the best sites in Scandinavia, set in a recreational wooded area alongside a sandy beach on the banks of the Baltic Sea, with the added bonus of the adjacent Eden Spa complex. Nallikari provides 200 pitches with electricity (some also have water supply and drainage), plus an additional 79 cottages to rent, 28 of which are suitable for winter occupation. Oulu is a modern town about 100 miles south of the Arctic Circle that enjoys long, sunny and dry summer days. The Baltic, however, is frozen for many weeks in the winter and the sun barely rises for two months. In early June the days are very long with the sun setting at about 11.30 pm and rising at 1.30 am! Nallikari, to the west of Oulu, is 3 km. along cycle paths and the town has much to offer. Nordic walking, with or without roller blades, seems to be a recreational pastime for Finns of all ages! Oulu hosts events such as the Meri Oulu Festival in July and forms the backdrop to the mind boggling, mime guitar playing world championships.

You might like to know
Activities on the beach include beach volleyball and nearby there are beach tennis courts.

☑ Beach on site
☐ Beach within 1 km.

☑ Sandy beach
☐ Blue Flag quality
☐ Lifeguard *(high season)*
☐ Sun lounger/deckchair hire
☐ Watersports
   (e.g. sailing, windsurfing)
☐ Snacks and drinks
☐ Sunshades
☐ Dogs allowed *(on the beach)*

Facilities: The modern shower/WC blocks also provide male and female saunas, kitchen and launderette facilities. Facilities for disabled visitors. Motorcaravan service point. Playground. Reception with café/restaurant, souvenir and grocery shop. TV room. WiFi. Bicycle hire. Off site: The adjacent Eden centre provides excellent modern spa facilities where you can enjoy a day under the glass-roofed pool with its jacuzzis, saunas, Turkish baths and an Irish bath. Fishing 5 km. Golf 15 km.

Open: All year.

Directions: Leave route 4/E75 at junction with route 20 and head west down Kiertotie. Site well signed, Nallikari Eden, but continue on, just after traffic lights, cross a bridge and take the second on the right. Just before the Eden Complex turn right towards Lerike and reception.
GPS: 65.02973, 25.41793

Charges guide

Per unit incl. 2 persons	€ 9,00 - € 18,00
extra person	€ 4,00
child (under 15 yrs)	€ 1,00
electricity	€ 4,00 - € 6,00

Been to any good campsites lately?
We have

You'll find them here...

The UK's market leading independent guides to the best campsites

...and, new for 2011, here...

101 great campsites, ideal for your specific hobby, pastime or passion

Want independent campsite reviews at your fingertips?

You'll find them here...

Over 3,000 in-depth campsite reviews at **www.alanrogers.com**

...and even here...

An exciting free app from iTunes and the Apple app store*

*available January 2011

Want to book your holiday on one of Europe's top campsites?

We can do it for you. No problem.

The best campsites in the most popular regions - we'll take care of everything

alan rogers ⟨⟩ travel

Discover the best campsites in Europe
with Alan Rogers

alanrogers.com
01580 214000

index

index

Associació de Càmpings
DE SANT PERE PESCADOR

Paradise under a blue sky

Discover Sant Pere Pescador's campsites

Located on the Costa Brava, Sant Pere Pescador sits between the sea and the mountains, part of the Empordà Natural Park. It's the only stretch on the Costa Brava with over 6 km of pristine sandy dunes, leading to the warm, shimmering waters of the Mediterranean. You'll find a choice of great family campsites, offering all kinds of activities, watersports, hiking, riding and cycling, as well as great swimming pools, restaurants and services.

Environmental conservation

The ACSPP campsites aim to protect the remarkable environment that surrounds them - many have achieved the EMAS certificate and ISO 1400.

www.acspp.org

Càmping Aquarius
Platja, s/n.
17470 Sant Pere Pescador. Girona
t: **(0034) 972 520 003**
f: **(0034) 972 550 216**
www.aquarius.es

Càmping La Ballena Alegre
17470 Sant Pere Pescador. Girona.
t: **(0034) 902 510 520**
f: **(0034) 902 510 521**
www.ballena-alegre.com

Càmping Las Dunas
17470 Sant Pere Pescador. Girona.
t: **(0034) 972 521 717**
f: **(0034) 972 550 046**
www.campinglasdunas.com

Càmping La Gaviota
Carretera de la Platja, s/n.
17470 Sant Pere Pescador. Girona.
t: **(0034) 972 520 569**
f: **(0034) 972 550 348**
www.lagaviota.com

Càmping Las Palmeras
Carretera de la Platja, s/n.
17470 Sant Pere Pescador. Girona.
t: **(0034) 972 520 506**
f: **(0034) 972 550 285**
www.campinglaspalmeras.com